# CAMBRIDGE LIBRARY COLLECTION

*Books of enduring scholarly value*

## Travel and Exploration

The history of travel writing dates back to the Bible, Caesar, the Vikings and the Crusaders, and its many themes include war, trade, science and recreation. Explorers from Columbus to Cook charted lands not previously visited by Western travellers, and were followed by merchants, missionaries, and colonists, who wrote accounts of their experiences. The development of steam power in the nineteenth century provided opportunities for increasing numbers of 'ordinary' people to travel further, more economically, and more safely, and resulted in great enthusiasm for travel writing among the reading public. Works included in this series range from first-hand descriptions of previously unrecorded places, to literary accounts of the strange habits of foreigners, to examples of the burgeoning numbers of guidebooks produced to satisfy the needs of a new kind of traveller - the tourist.

## The Cruise of the *Antarctic* to the South Polar Regions

The Norwegian businessman, shipping magnate and whaling entrepreneur Henrik Johan Bull (1844–1930) led the first expedition to make a confirmed landing on the Antarctic mainland, at Cape Adare, in January 1895. Bull's highly readable account of the expedition, published in 1896, reveals both the scientific and the commercial motivations for early Antarctic exploration. His voyage, financed by Svend Foyn, the inventor of the harpoon gun, was mainly for commercial purposes, to investigate reports of right whales in the Ross Sea. Bull, however, insisted on aiming for Antarctica, despite encountering technical problems after the vessel ran aground, and the preference of the ship's master for hunting seals to make the trip financially profitable. A part-time scientist on the expedition was Carsten Borchgrevink (1864–1934), who collected the first specimens of vegetation from the Antarctic, and later, with the Southern Cross expedition, set up the first winter base on the continent.

T0381850

Cambridge University Press has long been a pioneer in the reissuing of out-of-print titles from its own backlist, producing digital reprints of books that are still sought after by scholars and students but could not be reprinted economically using traditional technology. The Cambridge Library Collection extends this activity to a wider range of books which are still of importance to researchers and professionals, either for the source material they contain, or as landmarks in the history of their academic discipline.

Drawing from the world-renowned collections in the Cambridge University Library, and guided by the advice of experts in each subject area, Cambridge University Press is using state-of-the-art scanning machines in its own Printing House to capture the content of each book selected for inclusion. The files are processed to give a consistently clear, crisp image, and the books finished to the high quality standard for which the Press is recognised around the world. The latest print-on-demand technology ensures that the books will remain available indefinitely, and that orders for single or multiple copies can quickly be supplied.

The Cambridge Library Collection will bring back to life books of enduring scholarly value (including out-of-copyright works originally issued by other publishers) across a wide range of disciplines in the humanities and social sciences and in science and technology.

# The Cruise of the *Antarctic* to the South Polar Regions

Henrik Johan Bull

CAMBRIDGE UNIVERSITY PRESS

Cambridge, New York, Melbourne, Madrid, Cape Town,
Singapore, São Paolo, Delhi, Tokyo, Mexico City

Published in the United States of America by Cambridge University Press, New York

www.cambridge.org
Information on this title: www.cambridge.org/9781108041867

© in this compilation Cambridge University Press 2012

This edition first published 1896
This digitally printed version 2012

ISBN 978-1-108-04186-7 Paperback

This book reproduces the text of the original edition. The content and language reflect
the beliefs, practices and terminology of their time, and have not been updated.

Cambridge University Press wishes to make clear that the book, unless originally published
by Cambridge, is not being republished by, in association or collaboration with, or
with the endorsement or approval of, the original publisher or its successors in title.

# THE CRUISE OF THE 'ANTARCTIC'

The "Antarctic" among the Icebergs.

THE

# CRUISE OF THE 'ANTARCTIC'

*TO THE SOUTH POLAR REGIONS*

BY H. J. BULL

*WITH FRONTISPIECE BY W. L. WYLLIE, A.R.A., AND
ILLUSTRATIONS BY W. G. BURN MURDOCH*

EDWARD ARNOLD

LONDON                    NEW YORK
37 BEDFORD STREET         70 FIFTH AVENUE

1896

# PREFACE

I SHOULD never have ventured to offer the narrative of my Antarctic voyage in 1894-1895 to the British public if I had not received the valuable assistance of my cousin, Mr. J. C. Bull, of Bexley Road, Erith, Kent, in whose family circle most of this book has taken shape. Without the assistance of his English wife, Mrs. Edith Bull, as consulting oracle and dictionary in the choice of suitable words and phrases, the task would, however, have been beyond us. I must, therefore, be allowed to express my grateful sentiments to both for their assistance.

H. J. BULL.

TANDBERG, RINGERIKE,
    NORWAY.
*May,* 1896.

# CONTENTS

# LIST OF ILLUSTRATIONS

# CRUISE OF THE 'ANTARCTIC'

## CHAPTER I.

### *ORIGIN OF THE EXPEDITION.*

It is not pretended that the appearance of this book is justified by any extraordinary hardships or feats of endurance and fortitude on the part of the members of the late Antarctic Expedition, of which I had the honour to be the promoter and manager abroad ; but as we had the good fortune to penetrate to latitudes only passed by two previous explorers, Sir James Ross and Captain Weddell, and as we further succeeded in reaching the mainland of the great Antarctic Continent, never before trodden by human foot, I hope that my readers will find the history of the undertaking not wholly devoid of interest.

Our discovery in Antarctica of vegetation, hitherto believed non-existent, and the specimens detached from the rocks of the mainland, constitute the meagre additions to natural science gained by the expedition ; but our experiences in the Southern ice-fields, and our rough meteorological observations, recorded in my narrative, or in the accompanying extracts of the ship's log, may also be of some value to the scientific world, as well as to those who may contemplate further exploration in the same regions.

The report of our whaling and sealing will have some interest for practical men, and although we were spared, as already intimated, the physical sufferings from cold and privation at the price of which so many Arctic explorers have bought their fame, I hope that the story of our narrow escapes from shipwreck, our adventures amongst the ice, and in the hunting of whales and seals, may prove attractive even to the general reader.

Of my personal tribulations and disappointments before obtaining the support necessary for starting the enterprise, I will mention nothing beyond what is required for the sequence of the narrative.

About 1890, or a little earlier, serious efforts were made by the scientific bodies of Australia to raise funds for sending out an expedition to the Antarctic for scientific research, and negotiations were carried on for that purpose with the famous Swedish explorer, Baron Nordenskjold, who was asked to accept the leadership of the expedition.

Substantial amounts were privately subscribed, and with the various official grants promised, the total nearly reached the sum of £15,000 estimated to be required for the undertaking; but finally the plan fell through, as the interest shown by the colonies was not equal to overcoming the last difficulties. I was at this time engaged in one of the mercantile houses of Melbourne—Messrs. Trapp, Blair and Co. Having heard so much of the early whaling round the Australian coasts, and considering the comparatively small distance from Australia to the Antarctic, the idea struck me that an expedition on commercial lines would possibly find supporters amongst the speculative colonial business men. Having carefully studied various works by Antarctic explorers, notably those of Sir James Ross, I came to the conclusion that good business should result from such commercial enterprise, if the statements about the numerous Right or black whales given by Sir James proved correct. The price of whalebone at the time was higher than ever, so that the capture of only a few fish would amply repay the cost of outfit of an ordinary whaler. In the works referred to, seals were also described as very numerous in the Antarctic seas, and as I have in an earlier period of my life been personally interested in whaling as well as sealing vessels, I knew full well the exceptional profit that may with fair success be derived from this particular trade. The opening up of a whaling and sealing industry would mean a boon of no small extent to Australia in particular, as it would form a convenient outlet for numbers of unemployed labourers willing to work, of whom Australia has in these latter days had plenty, and to spare.

At the outset the press was the only medium I could employ to obtain public support for my idea. I derived only one advantage from my first letter to an evening paper, but it was not a small one; I thereby made the acquaintance of Sir Ferdinand (Baron) von Mueller, of botanical fame, who has ever since shown extreme kindness and goodwill towards me and my efforts in the cause of Antarctic exploration.

Some time afterwards I found the columns of the leading Melbourne paper open for my letters on the subject, and had the satisfaction of getting several replies in the same journal. Although the

writers fully agreed with me, and also signed
their names to their articles, I never got an
answer to my appeals to them for further com-
munications ; and I shall never forget a certain
day when I hunted Collins Street all over, from
west to east, to find one Mr. Miller, who gave his
address at number so and so, stating how deeply
he was interested in the question. In spite of
the most thorough search, no Mr. Miller of the
description I wanted was ever found. If he
should happen to read these lines, I must hereby
convey to him my best thanks for the pleasant
hours he gave me in my endeavours to run him
to earth.

Through the support which my then employer
gave to my advocacy of the Antarctic as a commercial field of operation, I had at one time fair
prospects in Melbourne of floating a company for
whaling and sealing purposes ; but the financial
crack of 1892 intervening, effectually destroyed
for the time being all hopes of success in Australia
of any enterprise of such a nature.

It goes against the grain to give up an idea
which has occupied one's thoughts by night and
day for years, but there was nothing for it ; with
the downfall of firm after firm, my heart and

hopes grew fainter and fainter, and with the closing of the doors of the eighteenth bank, it was only too easy to realize that every chance in Melbourne had vanished.

I had, however, always been in correspondence on the subject with my old friends in Norway, some of whom thought favourably of my plan, though without expressing an inclination to join actively in the enterprise. Thinking that a personal canvass might be more effective, I left Melbourne in February, 1893, and, soon after my arrival in Norway, paid my usual visit to Commander Svend Foyn, whom I had known for many years ; he was at the time an old man of eighty-four, and I never for one moment entertained a hope that he would at his age pioneer a venture of this kind. He was aware of my newspaper articles in Melbourne, and my correspondence with Norwegian whalers, and I had scarcely been with him five minutes when he started off on the Antarctic subject.

It goes without saying that my tongue was soon loosened, and the next moment the old man was rushing upstairs in his usual hurry, returning at the double quick with a large globe, on which I had to point out for him the open bay, stretching eastward of South Victoria Land as the most likely home of the Right whale. According to Sir James Ross, these whales were also plentiful in the vicinity of Possession Islands, and along the coast towards Cape North.

Commander Foyn without hesitation remarked, ' If Right whales are found South at all, they must be there,' adding, If you like to go back again, I will let you have one of my vessels if I can find a good captain.'

If I liked to go back again ! Yes, I should say so. But what dumbfounded me was the fact of this old gentleman of eighty-four settling in a short fifteen minutes what I had been vainly struggling to effect during the last three years. Many a day and night had I spent in writing pamphlets, estimates, and newspaper articles, without apparent progress towards the realization of my idea, when I suddenly found myself face to face with the man who could say, and did say, ' I will let you have the ship.' Shall I ever meet again a gentleman of his age (or thirty years his junior) so buoyant in spirit and quick of impulse as to consider and decide upon so large and venturesome an enterprise after a quarter of an hour's deliberation ?

# CHAPTER II.

*COMMANDER SVEND FOYN.*

THE man who thus in a moment undertook to find the means of realizing my ideas is so well known to thousands of British sailors and visitors to his whaling stations, and is withal so striking and generally interesting a personality, that I need hardly apologize for digressing from the immediate subject of my story in order to trace his life and character with a few brief touches.

I feel much satisfaction in thus doing homage to a great man, to whom I owe such a debt of gratitude, and to whose phenomenal energy and penetration of practical intellect the world owes the creation of an industry occupying thousands of hands at the present time, and capable in the future of employing thousands more, when his appliances are adopted outside his own country. It is much to be regretted that he is no longer

SWANTYPE

COMMANDER SVEND FOYN.

among the living; otherwise he might, with his usual—or, rather, unusual—perseverance, have continued the work so nobly begun for the exploitation of Antarctic waters. The news of his death in November, 1894, reached us on our return to Melbourne from the South Polar regions, and came as a severe blow to several members of the expedition, but particularly to me, who lost in him the truest and kindest of friends, one whom I can never hope to replace.

Svend Foyn was born in Tönsberg, Norway, in 1809. Like most boys of his time and position, he took to the sea, when about fourteen years of age, and in due time obtained the command of a vessel in the timber trade. His splendid physique, and corresponding mental gifts and energy, soon acquired for him a name as a particularly promising skipper. Anxious to extend his knowledge, he spent some time in England, in order to pick up enough of the language for his calling, a proceeding which was at that time a customary finish to the education of young Norwegian captains; but he thoroughly surprised his friends when one day, after mooring his vessel safely for the winter, he set off for Paris to tackle the French language as well, so as to be able to do his ship's business when in that country.

Paris can seldom have seen an earlier riser among its students. At four o'clock he commenced the wrestle with French grammar and its irregular verbs. As part of the reward for his enterprise, he would afterwards save the high and unreasonable brokers' fees imposed in those days on foreigners.

A ridiculous scene occurred on the first occasion when he entered his own vessel, and presented the manifest of his own composition at the Custom House. The jealous brokers around him suggested that it was not written by himself, and he was therefore asked by the officials to read it aloud. Keenly feeling the insult, he 'sang out' the manifest in such stentorian French that no work could proceed in the whole Custom House, and the officials had to beg of him to kindly desist, as there could be no further doubt as to his perfect mastery of the language.

The uninteresting lumber trade did not, however, suit his restless and adventurous spirit. At the end of the forties his attention was drawn to the lucrative seal-fisheries carried on by Scotch and German vessels in the Arctic seas, whilst

Norway at the same time was only represented by a few vessels of insignificant tonnage. He enlisted as mate on board a small sealing schooner ' to spy out the land.' On his return, he laid the keel of his first vessel with the assistance of his family. His first year as captain was, however, a terrible disappointment ; he came back practically with a clean ship. A time of trial and anxiety followed, sufficient to break any but the most determined spirit. The family resources were almost exhausted ; his townsmen listened coldly to his appeals, and the Government was in vain applied to for assistance, a thing which the old gentleman never forgot ; but through a successful intermediate voyage and ceaseless activity, he was, after all, enabled to start the following season for the icy regions of undoubted but fickle riches, from whence he this time returned with a full ship.

This event was the commencement of the extensive sealing trade to the Arctic seas from the southern ports of Norway.

Speculative merchants were not slow to follow in his wake, and a fleet of ships, employing upwards of a thousand men, soon brought fortunes to the happy owners, and a good living to the crews and their families. Remarkably good luck always accompanied the pioneer himself; year after year he came home with heavy cargoes of oil and sealskins.

The general stir and expansion caused in our little town by this sudden inrush of wealth and activity form some of the most exciting memories of my schooldays: the general uproar and disorder on 'signing-on day'; the feverish activity of fitting out; the great departure in February, after days of hard work in getting the vessels through the ice; then the months of external calm, but inward suspense and endless conjecture; at last, one day in early May, a thundering volley from the fjord; cries of 'There is Foyn, first again, full cargo!'; wild stampede to the shore by young and old; out in the boats (your own or someone else's) to board the ships, with their well-known green hulls down to load-line, and an oily, grinning, cheering crew. What days for all, what days for the young, and, alas! what days for schoolmasters, with half the classes suddenly stricken with colds, indigestion, or any other disease quickly put on and off!

In 1865 Mr. Foyn was already the possessor of a very considerable fortune, gained in his new enterprise.

To better compete with the Scotch sealers, he followed their example, and introduced steam-power in two of his ships. Unwilling to merely follow in the wake of others, he sent his vessels roaming all over the Arctic seas, discovering new sealing grounds, which have since his time been a kind of private hunting-field for Norwegian vessels.

But as the sealing trade settled down into monotonous success, Mr. Foyn again grew rest-less. With a fortune in the bank, he could now give his undivided attention to a matter which had long engrossed his mind, viz., the capture of the hitherto unconquered blue or finned whales, which at that time were found in large numbers round the coasts of Norway.

Here was an undertaking exactly to his mind. Americans, Danes, and at least one Englishman, had tried and failed to subdue these monsters, which, in addition to their incredible strength, offer their pursuers a further difficulty in the fact of their sinking when killed. Beyond the glory of succeeding where everyone else had failed, his shrewd business eye also perceived the immense wealth which would accrue to the man who could get the better of this hitherto unvanquished animal.

With characteristic determination, he altogether abandoned the Arctic seas, and left the sealing to his captains, in order to bend the whole of his energy and practical mind toward the solution of the new self-imposed crux. He speedily grasped and solved the lesser half of the difficulty—the power of the blue whale is such that the small boats sufficient for the capture of the Right whale are only toys when towed behind a wounded blue whale, and would in most cases promptly be dragged to the bottom, should the monster by good luck be killed. He therefore designed for the chase a small steamer, of such tonnage that the harpooned whale would tow it along without fear of breaking the line, and still of sufficient burden to quickly exhaust the animal, and to buoy it safely when killed.

The harpoon and gun, with its line, however, proved a tantalizing difficulty. Year after year was spent in failures and alterations suggested thereby. The battery of small guns, with which the poor whale was at first bombarded in vain, shrunk until the single huge bow-gun now generally used was developed, carrying a harpoon with an explosive bomb, weighing together about three-quarters of a hundredweight, and with a line attached two and a half to three inches in diameter.

To this terrible combination the blue whale had to succumb; but its development cost the inventor nearly five years of unceasing thought and labour, and a loss in experiments and failures estimated by him at about £20,000.

During this time he was his own engineer, designer, artillery officer, and mechanic, his chief assistant being a common blacksmith. Like many other self-made men of strong practical intellect, he looked upon scientific men and theorists with a feeling of suspicion, mingled with some disdain —a feeling which no doubt cost him a good proportion of the above £20,000.

Before the explosive bomb had been rendered perfect, the chase was dangerous in the extreme. Time after time came the news to our expectant town that a whale had been harpooned, but had freed himself after towing the vessel at express speed for eight to twelve hours. Mr. Foyn told me the story of the most exciting of these episodes, when a huge whale had been firmly harpooned, but not in a vital part. There was a gale blowing with heavy seas, in the teeth of which the animal towed the steamer at a speed of eighteen knots, by Mr. Foyn's estimation, although the engine went full speed astern, and a sail was set to increase the resistance. When a towing feat of twelve hours' duration over and under the water had left the monster's energy still un-diminished, even Mr. Foyn thought it best to cut the line. It is said that the crew compelled him to do so, but that I do not believe. A whale might conquer the old man, but no living crew —particularly at the time of his fullest vigour.

Having perfected his invention, he—as a shrewd man of business—obtained a patent for it, and thus for a long period enjoyed a lucrative monopoly, amassing a fortune, large even if measured by an English scale.

During the later years of his monopoly the annual catch sometimes exceeded a hundred large whales, realizing about £250 apiece, if we include the value, not only of the oil and bone, but also of the manure produced from the huge carcasses by machinery designed mainly by Commander Foyn.

When the monopoly ceased, his appliances were copied and used with such vigour from stations round the northern parts of Norway, and also in Iceland, that the catch in 1894 amounted to 1,528 animals, killed from forty-four steamers.

The industry at this time employed in all its branches more than a thousand hands.

Many visitors to the North Cape must have observed some of the small steamers in search or pursuit of their prey. Some of the animals reach a length of over ninety feet, and an approximate weight of eighty tons. They combine with their Titanic strength an agility astounding for such a bulk, and their chase should therefore be capable of rousing the jaded spirit of the most splenetic sportsman.

Commander Foyn's victory in his battle with the blue whale claims in one respect the interest of the naturalist. It forms the last chapter in the struggle of human intellect against brute force. Every other animal had long previously had to acknowledge the superiority of man.

The present chapter would assume the proportions of a volume, should I relate one tenth of the stories current in Norway of the old Commander. I must confine myself to a short sketch of his character, of which a fair impression will already have been received from the foregoing. His chief characteristics were a devotion to work and hatred of idleness, amounting to a passion ; intense and orthodox views of religion ; a will, energy, resourcefulness, administrative quality, and power of command over himself and others, which marked him out as a ruler of men and leader in large undertakings.

From the time when he, as a boy, assisted his mother with money obtained through the productions of his lathe, until the day on which he suddenly expired at the age of eighty-five, he pursued his daily work with an intensity which may be judged from the one fact that even at the zenith of prosperity he personally started his men at five in the morning, taking the lead in their labours throughout the day, and attending to his office work till late at night.

His hatred of waste, and the simplicity of his life and tastes, were truly Spartan.  At the whaling stations he would mess with the sailors, using one plate for the whole dinner, as is usual in the forecastle ; first soup with biscuits, then, say, herring and potatoes, with precious little to follow, if I know aright the dietary on board Norwegian vessels.

Whilst his annual donations of all kinds ran into thousands, his home life was not different from that of a middle-class Englishman of temperance proclivities, although no visitor to his house ever had reason to complain of lack of hospitality so long as luxuries were not expected.

His excellent wife was a true helpmate to a man of his extraordinary character. Until he was about seventy years of age, this good lady was his sole assistant in the transaction of his enormous business, without interference with her duties as the perfect housewife and the discreet distributer of innumerable gifts.

To ' eat bread in the sweat of his face until he returned to the ground ' were no idle words to him, of which I personally had an experience, very distressing at the time, but proving his unconquerable spirit as long as any spirit was left in him.

In his last years he suffered from fits, due to occasional failure of the heart's action. During one of our visits to Christiania on business, he suddenly fell down in one of these fits late at night, and the doctor who was called in stated that paralysis of the left side had set in, and that the case was apparently hopeless. I got him carried to the hospital, where he remained for hours in an unconscious state. When calling at three in the night, the patient was sleeping peacefully; at seven, I found the expected corpse

sitting up and dressed, laughing heartily at
my fright, and anxious to commence the day's
work so as to make up for lost time. The doctors
prevailed on him to stop till ten o'clock, when he
could not be detained any longer, but dragged me
round from place to place, jumping off tram-cars,
and hurrying in his usual way, utterly oblivious of
anything but the purposes of his visit. To follow
him up and down ladders into the ship's hold and
engine-room, across narrow planks in the docks,
etc., was, with my knowledge of his ailment, a
very uncomfortable task to me ; but the exercise
seemed particularly exhilarating to the octo-
genarian invalid.

In his lifetime, he distributed his large income
to a great extent in the support of the many
benevolent institutions and missions claiming his
interest; he was also ready to take the lead in
any new industrial enterprise which appeared to
him of national importance. At his death, the
greater portion of his fortune was willed to foreign
missions, and as I hold that the expedition of the
*Antarctic* may be classed among the latter, it was
a great comfort to me to feel that no relative of
his can complain of being robbed through the
pecuniary loss incurred by our voyage—the more

so as the heathen blacks will never realize their loss or bear us any ill will on account of their reduced wardrobe.

It would be very ungenerous to ascribe his strongly religious temperament merely to the dangers of his calling, although gratitude for hairbreadth escapes, and for the brilliant results of his labour, no doubt was a potent factor in it.

Of his narrow escapes little is known, as he rarely alluded to them himself, except when they had a comical side to tickle his sense of humour.

When helping his crew, as a young Captain, to set the foresail in the Bay of Biscay during a gale, a sea knocked him off his feet, and was carrying him over the railing, when the boatswain caught him round the legs, and hauled him back, with a popular Norwegian phrase, ' This time you are my pig, Foyn.' As long as he lived, it was his boast that he was the only man living who had dared to call Foyn a pig.

A whaling incident came, however, much nearer to a tragic ending. Accidents to life or limb are not uncommon when the harpooned whale runs out the coils of rope at lightning speed ; woe betide the man who stands in the way ! One day Mr. Foyn himself got his foot entangled in the whirring line, and disappeared over the railing like a flash, with the horror-struck crew standing helplessly by. Now, it is a case of the extremest rarity that a harpooned fin-whale ever slackens in his struggle when once caught; to the last gasp he rushes on, tons upon tons of agonized living matter. But this particular whale did check his rush for an instant, which sufficed for the drowning man to uncoil the rope and escape. Having swum to the steamer, and been pulled on board, the mate, half imbecile by his recent fright, could find no better greeting than, 'I—I am afraid you got wet, Captain,' a transition to comedy which nearly killed with laughing the man who had just escaped drowning and mutilation.

During the years when Mr. Foyn elaborated his explosive bomb, it is fair to assume that he every day took his life in his hands ; but nothing went off too prematurely, and therefore nothing will ever be known on this point.

To pretend that Mr. Foyn had no faults would be foolish; but I do not think it necessary to enter into a description of them—the more so as most of them formed a kind of necessary counterpart to his virtues. A man who was accustomed to find his own opinions on practical subjects almost universally correct naturally became rather intolerant of the opinions of others.    His own immense capacity for work often made him unjust towards weaker vessels.    His determination often assumed the shape of obstinacy, and sometimes took amusing forms.

When, for instance, he took it into his head that his taxes were assessed unjustly, he at once started building a new house outside the town borders.    When nearly completed, the Council quietly extended the border so as to include the new residence; but Mr. Foyn as quietly pulled down the house, re-erecting it on the other side of the harbour.

If the foregoing pages have not given my readers the impression that the world lost in Svend Foyn a unique industrial pioneer of striking practical intellect, a giant among men, a true descendant of his Viking ancestors, the fault is that of my pen, not that of the man.    On no person could the title ' Commander' be bestowed with more appropriateness—a man who possessed every physical and mental quality calculated to impress the minds of his followers with his superiority, and to fill them with his own enthusiasm for the work in hand ; a man who ever took more than his full share of the hardest and most common labour, without for a moment losing sight of the general plan of operations.

Like other strong and particularly outspoken men, he caused some opposition and soreness in his lifetime ; that his nation, however, understood his value as a man and a citizen was proved by the universal expressions of sympathy and grief at the news of his very sudden death, due to the heart complaint already referred to.

# CHAPTER III.

## THE STEAM-WHALER 'ANTARCTIC.'

HAVING found the man willing to pay for the expedition, it remained to find a suitable ship. All the larger steam-sealers were at the time absent on their Arctic cruise, and to await their return would have endangered the chances of an expedition in the same year. Mr. Foyn therefore finally bought a steam-sealer retired from active service, and subsequently rebaptized it the *Antarctic*.

This small handy ship of 226 registered tons net was built in Norway about 1872, and put in the Arctic sealing trade, where she did good work during a succession of years. When Commander Foyn took her over, we found the vessel neglected in many respects, and requiring a thorough overhaul of hull and engines, which was given her in Tönsberg and Christiania.

The original engine had only one high-pressure cylinder, and would have consumed too much coal for an Antarctic voyage; it was therefore converted into a compound tandem engine, which proved particularly economical with regard to consumption of fuel. The engine was capable of developing forty-five nominal horse-power, which gave the vessel a speed of six knots an hour in calm weather; in spite of this rather slow performance, the immense advantage of an auxiliary engine was fully appreciated when pounding through the ice-pack or navigating among icebergs. The engine and boiler with bunkers occupied the whole after-portion of the vessel, excepting a few compartments set apart for stores.

Her hull was built on the ordinary lines of sealing vessels—that is, with timbers of extraordinary dimensions, double outer planking from keel to deck, besides a third sheathing of greenheart or other hard wood reaching from her bilges upwards beyond the load-line, designed to receive the direct grinding and pounding of the ice.

Her bows were specially protected and strengthened outside by iron bands, half an inch thick, laid close together, and inside by the usual immense timber and iron fastenings.

In her lower hull she carried thirty-eight iron tanks, capable of storing about 150 tons of oil, and moulded to fit the hull, thus adding greatly to the strength of the vessel in case of violent collisions with heavy ice.

The rig was that of the usual barque, but in order to increase the speed of her weighty hull in the light trade-winds, and to save coal, royals were added for the occasion. It requires half a gale to drive these heavy vessels at their best speed ; under such conditions we frequently, in the tempestuous Forties, found her spinning along at the rate of nearly twelve miles per hour.

We were provided with seven boats of the usual sealing type, which ultimately proved too clumsy for effective use in Right, or sperm, whaling.

The forecastle was under deck, divided by a partition between the foremen and the common hands. The cabin was on deck, and just large enough to afford very cramped accommodation for the Captain, the two mates, and the writer. The engineers had their quarters adjoining the engine-room.

The want of space compelled us to stow our large stores of gunpowder, guns, explosive shells, cartridges, etc., in a manner more picturesque than safe or soothing to nervous constitutions. For some time I shared my crib with a number of powder-kegs, uncomfortable neighbours to a heavy smoker.

To detail all the necessaries of the outfit for a whaling and sealing ship equipped for the Antarctic would be tedious to anyone but the practical reader; suffice it to say that we carried eleven guns for firing harpoons with explosive shells from the vessel or her boats, numbers of harpoons of various weights, with bombs and shells, rifles and cartridges for sealing, and provisions for nine months for a crew of thirty-one all told. When everything was on board, including 210 tons of coal, the vessel was down to her load-mark.

Our coals were stored in the oil-tanks, by which arrangement we were enabled to carry a sufficient quantity for a very protracted cruise. The re-filling of our bunkers from the tanks was a labour of some magnitude, owing to our primitive tackle, and in consequence no great amount of spare time was ever wasted by the crew.

Some of the tanks were also used for storing

water ; nevertheless, the consumption proved so
rapid that we had to catch and save the rain in
the tropics to ensure a full supply.

Mr. Sanne, a whaling skipper, who had just
returned from a cruise to the south of Cape
Horn, was originally engaged as Captain of the
*Antarctic*, but an unfortunate misunderstanding
ended in the cancellation of his contract by Mr.
Foyn, and Mr. L. Kristensen, of Tönsberg, took
his place.

In my opinion this appointment was unfortunate,
as Captain Kristensen, though possessed of some
experience in the Bottle-nose trade in open waters,
had had but little practice in other whaling, and
in sealing and navigation in the ice.

Our inexperience in the organization of exploring
expeditions also led us into a mistake.   My position towards the Captain was not sufficiently clearly
defined for me to feel it within my power to order
or command the carrying out of alterations or
innovations, however important in my opinion,
when they might be considered to strictly belong
to the domain of the nautical leader ; my sugges-
tions and advice in such cases received very
scant consideration, to the great detriment of
our venture.   Where the field of action lies

14,000 miles away from home, it is absolutely
necessary that one will should dominate, and it
is no comfort to me now to feel that our faulty
arrangements as to authority also relieved me of
much responsibility in respect of the final result.

As I had for years made Antarctic and Southern
whaling and sealing my study, it was galling in
the extreme to find myself powerless to avert
many of our disasters, however clearly I had
foreseen them and warned our nautical leader in
time to prevent them.

Our first mate had a good knowledge of Arctic
navigation, and Captain Bernhard Jensen, who
for seventeen years had pursued his calling as a
whaler and sealer in the North, was so eager for
adventure that he joined our vessel as second
mate, and did splendid service ; his experience
and cheerfulness under the most disheartening
circumstances stood us in good stead.  His great
sorrow in life to this day is that Mr. Nansen
could not find room for him among his crew, and
from this it will be understood that his spirit was
of the kind required for an adventurous expedition
such as ours.

The chief engineer was equally untiring in the
discharge of a particularly arduous duty throughout

the voyage, and the crew bore themselves in a praiseworthy manner, especially when it is considered that most of them naturally joined us in order to make money, and that the ultimate commercial failure of the expedition meant serious loss and disappointment to every man amongst them, their pay depending to a great extent on our net profits.   When, in 1894—in obedience to our orders and mission—we deliberately turned our backs on the hunting-grounds, where the previous season had brought us a good cargo during a few weeks' sealing, the crew as a whole cheerfully entered into the spirit of the undertaking, and, in spite of the subsequent disappointment, not a murmur ever reached me from the forecastle.

For the edification of those of my readers who may contemplate similar expeditions, I give below the approximate cost of our vessel and outfit. Our inexperience of undertakings of this nature led us into serious mistakes as regards equipment, which will be described as we found them out to our cost—mistakes which in some measure are responsible for the disappointing monetary result of the venture.

The errors in our provisioning were more

annoying than serious. Nominally, we were equipped for a voyage of nine months' duration ; but our supplies were so unequally provided that five months at sea were enough to exhaust, or nearly exhaust, many of our necessaries, whilst leaving us with a superabundance of others. Had we pushed on towards the great bay during the first season, and happened to be frozen in, the next summer would have found us alive—with good luck—but most certainly in a very attenuated condition—unless, indeed, we could have killed a few small whales for winter consumption, the flesh of young whales forming a food the excellence of which must be practically tried to be appreciated.

| | £ |
|---|---|
| The vessel was bought for about   .   .   . | 2,000 |
| Alterations to hull, engine and boiler cost about   . | 500 |
| New blubber digesters   .   .   .   . | 180 |
| Guns, harpoons, and shells   .   .   .   . | 200 |
| Harpoon and other lines   .   .   .   . | 210 |
| Alterations to masts and rigging, including new sails, several new yards, etc.   .   .   .   . | 310 |
| Provisions for thirty-one men during nine months, at 1s. 1½d. per man per day   .   .   . | 470 |
| Wages during the same time .   .   .   . | 600 |
| Insurance on vessel (6 per cent.)   .   .   . | 200 |
| Insurance on equipment   .   .   .   . | 30 |
| Two hundred tons of coal   .   .   .   . | 150 |
| Total   .   £4,850 | |

Or with divers expenses not enumerated above, say £5,000.

With the exception of £550 found by Messrs. Tho. Joh. Heftye and Sons, of Christiania, the expenses of the expedition were borne by Commander Foyn. My own small contribution derived its only importance (to me) from the fact that it represented my little all—and more.

# CHAPTER IV.

### THE START.—TRISTAN D'ACUNHA.

AFTER weeks of bustle and hurry with the outfit, we finally got under steam from Tönsberg on September 20, 1893, giving a parting cheer to Mr. Foyn, who had personally superintended everything, and sped us on our way.

The start was made so late in the year that our chances, both of successful whaling and of penetrating to the Great South Victoria Bay during the same season, were seriously impaired.

After a day spent in preparing for sea, and restoring something like order to our heaped-up decks, the pilot left us, and we set out on our adventurous quest. What would the next twelvemonth bring us ?

The beginning was not particularly auspicious. Our progress was slow on account of adverse and strong winds, and much of our new gear did not come out well from its early trial.

On the 27th of the month we called at Deal to
rectify the worst omissions in the way of small
stores. Off Beachy Head our jib-boom broke, but
happily the fore-topgallant mast did not follow
suit, and the damage was therefore quickly re-
paired.

Later on the fore-topgallant yard carried
away. Our new sails did not set well, and consequently did not assist us much when close-
hauled.

Madeira was sighted on October 16, after a
tedious voyage and contrary winds. On the 19th
we could at last square our yards to a fair breeze
and ease the engine, which had practically been
at work since our weighing the anchor.

On the 21st we ran into the harbour of Las
Palmas, Grand Canary, to replenish our coal, and
also, we hoped, to get a sight of the interesting
town, with its old cathedral, luxuriant gardens,
and tropic life. But this was not to be. Having
no sanitary pass—a thing forgotten in our hurried
start—the harbour police treated us as a floating
leper colony, and ordered us ignominiously outside
the breakwater. The exchange of documents
took place with the aid of a long pole, and the
elaborate care and truly Spanish solemnity with

which our papers were disinfected in sulphur
smoke by the police were highly diverting to a
crew arriving direct from the healthiest country in
the world.

After stowing forty-one tons of coal, and some
further exchange of papers through the medium of
the hospitable pole, we steamed away before a fair
and freshening breeze, leaving cathedral and town
unexplored behind us, and soon also the parched-
up island itself, while the wind increased till we
made six to seven knots under sail alone. When
sailing five knots, slow ahead with the engine
would add about one and a half knots to the speed
of our heavy vessel; sailing seven to eight knots,
the propeller was of little assistance.

A mysterious leak, which we were unable to
locate, had been a worrying trouble since our
start. It varied greatly in degree, and was
already so serious that we should hardly have
dared to proceed but for our trusty steam-pump.

*November* 2.—Lat. N. 6°. Slow progress.
Trade winds variable or absent. Great heat.
Our water not good. The butter, 'our best
drinkable,' as on Mark Twain's voyage.

*November* 6.—Crossing the line on the 22°
W. long. Fresh S.E. trade wind.

*November* 8.—Lat. S. 6°. Speed without engine seven and a half knots. Our vessel already troubled with barnacles, hindering progress.

Our preparations to receive the whales and seals when met with are now fairly complete ; four guns are mounted on the forecastle deck, three boats hanging in their davits, ready to lower when we meet the Right or sperm whales round Tristan d'Acunha. Our coals have shrunk alarmingly during the prolonged steaming ; there are to-day only about 130 tons left, counting the 41 tons from Las Palmas ; every economy must be practised.

*November* 16.—Lat. S. 24°. Fair winds ; good progress. Our topgallant sails have been standing since we left Las Palmas, except during an occasional calm, when the engine has had to do all the work.

*November* 21.—Lat. S. 33°. Getting into the westerly trade winds. Simultaneously with the change of wind comes the stirring cry of 'Whales ahead!' from the look-out ; all torpor is gone, and everywhere is excitement and commotion. The vessel is dodged about after the three fish, but the high wind prevents us from coming within striking distance, and after a time it is also evident that our whales are 'finners' (finned whales), and of no value to us.

We fell in with several large schools of whales in this latitude, but all of them finners, and therefore of no interest to us with our special outfit.

While flying proudly along yesterday, a full-rigger and a four-master hove in sight, and tore past our humbled craft at a speed of eleven to twelve knots. The change in temperature is considerable with the new direction of the wind. From 88° F. in the N.E. trade wind, the thermometer has now fallen to 66° F.

*November* 24.—Sighted the conical mountain-top of Tristan d'Acunha, 37° 5′ 50″ S. lat., 12° 16′ 40″ W. long., our next place of call for whaling news.

On drawing near to the iron-bound coast, the swell was found to be too great for us to land, but a boatload of young islanders soon came on board, and quickly displayed an unparalleled genius for begging and barter ; nothing—'from a needle to an anchor'—came amiss to them. In exchange for some bread, rice, and grain, we obtained a quantity of fish and a living sheep. The former appeared to be in the main identical with the Australian species of old personal acquaintance—schnapper, sea-perch, and a single barracouta. One among our visitors, of course, required a bottle of wine 'for his sick mother.' This plea will be met with in connection with spirituous desires among all nations since the time of Noah.

The eagerness for barter and begging is explained by the fact that cereals form a very precarious crop on the island, rendering the inhabitants dependent on vessels passing or calling for bread-stuffs, rice, etc., as well as for all manufactured articles.

The statements by our new friends that Right whales had been seen in numbers round the island during the last days filled us with hope and excitement; but I have since developed a suspicion that their statements were less founded on truth than on a desire to keep us with them, so long as we had anything to barter or give away. At any rate, we did not meet with a single Right or sperm whale during our stay, nor on our passage from Tristan to Kerguelen Islands.

In spite of the heavy weather, a landing was effected next morning under the lee of the island, which has no bay or harbour of any kind, but is protected by an enormous belt of sea-weed from the direct swell. We met all the inhabitants decked out in their best finery in honour of our presence. A general holiday is taken by old and young on such occasions, so complete that no assistance could be got that day in filling water, etc.

We called on old Captain Higgin, an American whaler, who for more than forty-two years had been living in contentment with his family on this remote volcanic rock, lost in the ocean waste more than a thousand miles away from the nearest mainland. In his active whaling days he found enough to do among the Right whales round Tristan from September to December. In the latter month he generally went south and east to Goughs and Crozet Islands, returning, he said, one year from the latter place with full cargo—1,900 casks of oil. With the 700 obtained from the hunting round Tristan, and counting in eight tons of whalebone, the value of his catch during this 'bumper' harvest of the sea may be calculated.

Although too late for effective whaling at Tristan, he reckoned that we should be able to do well round Prince Edward's, Crozet, Kerguelen, and Heard Islands, and was kind enough to give us much valuable information.

As this group of interesting islands has already been several times described, notably by the members of the *Challenger* Expedition, I will not weary my readers with a long description of Queen Victoria's smallest colony, over which our worthy American holds patriarchal sway.

The main island, nearly circular, is about twenty miles in circumference, and, like the smaller members of the group, Nightingale and Inaccessible Islands, of volcanic origin. Its mountain-peak is 8,340 feet high, the shores rising precipitously to a height of 1,000 to 2,000 feet in most places, and landing is only possible on the lee-side in anything like heavy weather. The population on the main islands consists now of only fifty-nine souls, living a life of fair contentment and rude comfort. A number of cattle, pigs, goats, and sheep are reared on the tussock and other grasses which cover the dells and plateaus throughout the year. Vegetables also thrive exceedingly, but grain is a precarious crop, as already stated, on account of the heavy gales to which these, as well as all the other islands of the South Atlantic, are exposed ;

but for these gales, and the frequently accompanying rain, the climate would be pleasant, the summer heat being tempered by the fresh wind that blows most of the time.

Besides the natural increase of the population, the number of inhabitants is occasionally augmented by shipwrecked mariners. A daughter of Captain Higgin was, for instance, married to the second mate of a large English vessel that was wrecked in broad daylight close to the island some months before our visit, the Captain being drunk at the time, and drowned in leaving the ship. The marriage (as is the case with all ministerial functions in the colony) was solemnized by Captain Higgin. A Government vessel calls at Tristan once a year, when an ordained clergyman re-celebrates Captain Higgin's ministerial acts, although the young people referred to appeared superabundantly happy without any official restamping of the primitive bond.

A Norwegian sailor lived for eight years in the colony, and married there, but ultimately left with his wife for the old home.

The language of the islanders is good English, but their dusky faces and un-English features betray the mixture of many races.

Ten years ago a terrible accident carried away nearly the whole of the young islanders at one stroke. Returning from a visit to a large vessel, the boat capsized with them, fifteen in number. Most of them got up on the bottom of the craft, but were too far away for assistance to reach them from the shore, whilst no effort of any kind to save them was made from the vessel ; the whole of the struggling party ultimately went down under the eyes of their families. It is poor comfort to know that Captain Higgin reported the matter to the Home Authorities, and that the captain of the vessel referred to was punished for his dastardly conduct.

No certain news could be got in reference to the seven black whales reported as having been noticed close under the shore, and we decided therefore to make sail without further loss of our precious time. Midsummer was fast approaching, and we were still hopeful of being able to penetrate to South Victoria Land before the close of the Antarctic summer.

We made sail on November 27. The wind soon increased to a gale of N.N.W., and with the course laid for Prince Edward's Island, the *Antarctic* soon sped away from mist-enveloped

Tristan at the rate of ten miles an hour. A number of whale-spouts were observed, but none belonging to black or sperm whales.

*December* 4.—The first large iceberg hove in sight in 40° 41′ S. lat., 15° E. long.; another was sighted shortly afterwards. We have made famous progress, the speed of our heavy vessel at times reaching eleven knots before the gale, which has shifted from N.N.W. to S.W., but allowed us to run or reach continuously. In the tremendous sea and wind met with on our voyage to Kerguelen, our little vessel proved herself a real duck, negotiating every breaking wave in a business-like manner. The squall, striking her with incredible force, appears to lift her bodily out of the sea. As she dives into the trough, her lee-rail is next flung under, the deck being often flooded from fore to aft; but each time she rises gracefully, and with an ease that is highly comforting to you as you lie at night in the berth, the narrowness of which you now appreciate for the first time.

After a few days of this violent plunging, you get more accustomed to the complicated motions necessary to preserve a balance, and can faintly appreciate the wild beauty of the well-named

The Roaring Forties.

'roaring Forties.' The endless succession of green
or gray-black mountainous billows, their breaking
crests, which are blown into shreds by the squall,
and carried through the rigging with a shrieking
and howling as of loosened demons, the flying
storm-rent clouds, and frequent mist and rain,
make a picture supremely grand in its own way.
With the addition of icebergs and darkness, however, I confess that a beauty of a milder type
would have been sufficient for me, who had never
before in person realized the astounding violence
of a gale in Southern latitudes, and the rapidity
with which a calm will change into a hurricane,
and the latter into a calm once more. My relief
when the day broke, or the barometer appeared
to rise in earnest, was consequently very heartfelt,
whilst the hardened sailors took everything as 'in
a day's work.'

During the intermittent spells of calm weather,
albatross fishing and shooting formed the Captain's
amusement; large numbers of petrels, gulls, and,
as a rule, Cape pigeons, enlivened the scenery.
Whales of the finned variety continue to be seen
almost daily.

*December* 12.—Sighted Marion, and later on
Prince Edward's Island, the top of the former

snow-covered; the sharply conical shape of the mountains reveals their volcanic origin. Landing is impossible at present, on account of the storm on the bayless shore, with its range of bold dark cliffs. The season is already so advanced that we dare not heave to and await a change of weather; we therefore tear along before the gale towards Crozet Islands.

The temperature of the air is now only 47° F., of the water 49° F., and the cold nights are felt severely after our tropical passage.

*December* 15.—According to our reckoning and observations, we are abreast of Penguin Island, of the Crozet Group; but clouds and mist hide the land, of which the hundreds of penguins playing round the vessel give early warning. We steer for Possession Island, and in the afternoon we are so near as to see and hear the breakers, the shore itself being invisible behind the shroud of vapour. Soon afterwards a good view of the south coast is obtained, with Ship Bay; between us and the latter ugly breakers are observed, although not marked on any chart, to which fact the attention of cartographers is hereby drawn.

At sundown we are favoured with a sight of the mountainous Possession and East Island, with

THE MIST IS RENT FOR A FEW MINUTES.

towering basaltic cliffs, against which the breakers
make unceasing but vain assault; the mist hanging over them is rent for a few minutes, and rolled
up around the 4,000 feet high mountain-tops in
heavy cloud-banks, which are tinted in rainbow
colours by the sun as he dips below the horizon—
a brilliant spectacle, only too fleeting.

Large numbers of penguins continue to sport
round the vessel, and myriads of these birds crowd
the ledges and escarpments of the rocks wherever
there is standing-room and the shore is accessible.

Thousands of petrels, gulls, and albatross add
to the peculiar bird-life of the islands.

No whales useful to us, however, are to be seen,
and landing is difficult; so we continue running
before the favourable gale for Kerguelen Islands,
where our chances of whaling and sealing are the
fairest. We have met with no icebergs except
the two already mentioned, and one source of
anxiety during the night has therefore been super-
fluous. The days are lengthening, and the four
to five hours' night is frequently illuminated by
the sailor's trusty companion, the moon.

During our journey from Marion, we have passed
the enormous floating islands of weed described
in the records of all previous navigators of this

region.    Numbers of whales have been seen during our passage to Kerguelen, most of them apparently finners, others quite strange to our men, but all of them useless to us with our present whaling gear, which is not suitable for the killing of anything but Right or sperm whales.

# CHAPTER V.

*KERGUELEN OR DESOLATION ISLANDS.*

*December* 19.—Sighted Benedet Island, of the
Kerguelen Group, in the morning, and ran along
the southern coast with a fair wind and a clear
sky.   Our intention was to call at these islands in
order to look for seals, but more particularly to
fill water preparatory to our going south and
commencing our attack on the ice—an attack
which subsequent events compelled us to delay
for a twelvemonth.

The volcanic mountain-tops reach a height of
6,000 feet, and were covered with snow, although
midsummer was already at hand.   With the lofty
ranges and numerous towering conical peaks, the
first view of Kerguelen was very imposing,
although severe and barren.   For miles the shore
is barricaded with high basaltic cliffs with bold
headlands, like Crozet Island ; and where the

4

range is broken by an occasional valley, the same teeming bird-life is met with. The penguins along these more accessible rocks, and the shores of the bays, are countless, and the scene of animation in the rookeries, now that the young birds are able to follow their parents, is perfectly bewildering.

We were unfortunately without a special chart of the land, and could not therefore penetrate with confidence into the many narrow firths which nearly cut through the island, but had to feel our way cautiously into Greenland Harbour, where we anchored towards evening in beautiful sunshine and calm. The Captain must needs go ashore the same evening to see what the land offers in the way of game. We soon heard shot upon shot, and were looking forward to a welcome change in the *menu* for supper, when our attention was drawn to objects on the opposite shore, which with the telescope were soon made out to be seals of a kind and size unknown to our Arctic fishermen.

Two boats were lowered in feverish haste, and the first sea-elephants were brought on board in the moonlight. The Captain's firing had also been at these animals, of which numbers had been met with along the shores.

The boats were ordered to be ready at two

o'clock the next morning, the near prospect of a good cargo driving away the desire for sleep that night. Tales of previous adventures, and speculation as to what awaited us in the morning, kept most of us very wide awake.

Next day every man, excepting the cook and engineer, was ashore, and employed in shooting and skinning the poor elephants, or in the more laborious task of dragging the skins and blubber to the shore and getting them on board.

About 350 were shot during the next two days, many of enormous size, yielding from three to four casks of blubber per animal. Their very size and weight made the labour connected with the capture particularly arduous. The four men belonging to each boat-party were sometimes unable to turn the dead seal over for skinning, and had to be assisted by their comrades. The skin and blubber together weighed in some cases more than six or seven hundredweight, which had to be dragged over stone and tussock to the shore, and then into the boats, which were frequently unable to approach the land closely on account of the extraordinary growth of sea-weed and the surf. In many places the kelp actually filled the entire harbours.

We found that the seals often travelled far inland, and then we had to drive them out of the deep hollows which constituted their hearth and home, in order that they might carry their own skin and blubber for us to the shore.  In one case the men were able to float the skins from the higher land down a small stream, and so reach the boats with them.

The details of seal-hunting are so particularly nauseating that I will spare my readers an exhaustive description.  The elephant must die that we may live.  This can be our only excuse for the slaughter of a particularly innocent and defenceless animal.

The crew of a sealing vessel, when engaged in actual capture, have to undergo exertions and privations of the severest kind.  Uncertainty as to how long the animals will stay necessitates that the work shall proceed as long as the men can stand.  No regular time for meals or sleep is possible, and a day's gale interrupting the work comes rather like a relief than otherwise.

The sportsman can find nothing attractive in the capture of the kind of seals we met with. They generally look on with quiet curiosity and interest at the preparations for their own execution by rifle bullet or pickaxe. Where the herd is numerous, the slaughter of a portion may cause the rest to be uneasy, but in no case will an elephant ashore try to defend itself, and in very few cases did they make a serious attempt to regain the water. When attacked at sea, on the other hand, they are said to defend themselves or their young with ferocity and intelligence, and have been known to keep parties from landing by manœuvring between the shore and the boat. The shores round Greenland Harbour and its branches were soon cleared of seals, which compelled us to change our field of operations.

Before getting away, we got our first lesson in Kerguelen hurricanes.

The rapidity with which these arise, and their incredible violence, are described so graphically in the reports by Sir James Ross and others that we had no excuse for being unprepared. The books of sailing directions are also full of warnings in this respect. As an illustration of the force of the wind, it will be remembered that one of Ross's men was lifted bodily off his feet and blown into the water during a squall; whilst it was at times necessary for the men ashore to lie down flat to avoid being similarly carried away.

As a nervous landsman, however, my representations of the necessity to prepare for sudden gales by rigging down our royal and topgallant yards on making the harbour had been somewhat scornfully rejected.  When, therefore, the danger-signal (the steam-whistle) sang out on the afternoon of December 22, calling the boat-parties on board, our state of unpreparedness, and the resulting confusion, nearly brought our expedition to an untimely end.  The vessel drifted before her anchor in spite of the engine going full ahead. The crew, with their heavy boats, could only reach us with the utmost difficulty—one party under our lee was, in fact, unable to stem the wind and sea, and had to spend the night ashore in much discomfort, as the Kerguelen cabbage is poor eating in a raw state, and the night air distinctly cool.

Meanwhile, all hands on board were struggling for dear life to extricate the second anchor from its too snug berth, and when at last it could be let go, we had only a few more fathoms to drift.  The two anchors held, and the danger was over, by good luck, when the storm moderated towards daybreak.  But with true Norwegian stubbornness —so admirable in the right, so aggravating in the wrong place—no rigging down of the yards and

general snugging of the vessel was even now decided upon. And so ended, in vain, our first lesson.

The excitement of our discovery of elephants
has prevented us from paying much attention to
the strange land which we are despoiling of its
children; but while our tanks are being emptied
of coals to give room for blubber, and the latter is
separated from the skins, there is time to look
round. A lengthy description of Kerguelen
would be out of place, as the records left us
by Sir James Ross, the Rev. Perry, and other
members of the *Challenger* Expedition, are so exhaustive as to require little amplification.

The enormous distance of the islands from any
mainland (upwards of 3,000 miles), their forbidding and sterile aspect from the sea, and the
generally dismal climate, explain why Captain
Cook named the group Desolation Islands—a
particularly fitting name, especially when the land
is made during one of the gales that rage for
three weeks out of every four, accompanied by
rain or snow even at midsummer. During our
stay, in the warmest month of the year, the
mountain-sides were covered with snow for a
considerable distance, and the weather, as a rule,
was raw and cold.

On the other hand, the climate varies little all the year round. During Sir James's stay in mid-winter, the conditions of atmosphere and vegetation were practically as we found them in midsummer. When the firths are entered, the grim aspect of the land changes very much for the better. The shores and valleys are frequently covered with high succulent grasses and plants, among which is the well-known Kerguelen cabbage. At present the rabbits alone benefit by the vegetation, on which large herds of sheep and cattle could be fed, as it is for the most part perennial; and the snow never covers the lower portion of the land for more than a few days at a stretch.

As the island also forms a good centre for whaling and sealing, and, finally, as it contains workable layers of coal, it is to be regretted that France should lately have shown a disposition to render effective her previous nominal possession of this interesting and prospectively valuable land, which has so far been in frequent, if somewhat intermittent, occupation by British sailors or British colonists from the Cape.

Numerous skeletons of whales along the shores of south-eastern harbours, fragments of blubber-caldrons, casks, ships' timber, and ropes, and even parts of houses, etc., met with in some sheltered places, testify to the previous importance of Kerguelen as a whaling and sealing station. According to Sir James Ross, several hundred vessels, chiefly American, collected at certain times of the year in search of the Right and sperm whale round the islands. The batteries of caldrons prove that fishing was frequently carried out by land-parties, who remained ashore for longer periods, ' trying out ' their blubber, and shipping it from time to time.

As the Right and sperm whales have of late become so rare as to render their capture—at least, with sailing ships and old appliances—a very precarious living, the future whaler, choosing Kerguelen as a centre, must look for his profits to the many varieties of finned whales now left to roam about undisturbed in large schools. I will, however, return to this subject when summing up the experience gained during the present expedition. At the same time I will give my views on the important future of sealing in Southern latitudes, an industry which must of necessity be intermittent and criminally wasteful in character so long as it is not controlled in a reasonable manner by internationally accepted regulations, as

in the Arctic seas, with a view to giving the
seals a chance of reproducing their kind.   The
incredible number of fur seals and sea-elephants
met with in Kerguelen, South Georgia, and the
South Shetlands, before they were nearly all
slaughtered during a few seasons of insane killing, prove the capacity of Antarctic waters to
maintain an enormous stock of these animals.

*December* 24 *to* 26.—The days before Christmas had been spent in clearing our decks, which
were nearly filled with the skins and blubber,
boiling the latter, etc.   Christmas Day was celebrated in company with the natives : thousands
of gulls, penguins, petrels, numbers of teal and
other varieties of duck ; the latter assisted us too
' materially ' for their own good in the celebration,
and proved excellent eating, even better than a
white species of bird, very similar in appearance
to our Norwegian ptarmigan, which occurred in
large numbers, and seemed to live on plants and
eggs ; their extreme tameness—they could be
taken with the hands—was a proof that many
years had elapsed since the departure of the last
resident sealers.

As they were reported to be feasting on the
seal carcases, their relationship to the ptarmigan

could not be so great as their appearance led us
to suppose, the more so as they kept their white
plumage in summer; the birds were in fact the
interesting *chionis* or sheath - bill described by
other visitors to Kerguelen.

The rabbit colony was also called upon to play
a part at our feast, where the *menu* was consequently both dainty and varied, including a
bastard 'cream porridge' made with flour, water,
and eight pounds of butter.

The cessation of work on December 25 and 26
was extremely acceptable to the men, worn out
by the last days' incessant labour and excitement.
The national colours floating from under the gaff
lent a fair appearance of Christmas festivity to
the vessel, but the traces of recent slaughter were
too many, and the prospect of future sealing too
near and too exciting, to induce a proper feeling
of 'peace on earth' within us.

The sudden stoppage of our mysterious and
worrying leak was a most welcome Christmas
gift; floating blubber or sea-weed must have been
sucked in and have stopped it; as the water had
lately been coming in at the rate of twelve inches
per watch, the pumping had been almost unceasing. Alas! a few days later the leak

appeared again as suddenly as it had vanished, and increased in degree up to fourteen inches of water per watch.

The animal life on the island was a source of never-ending interest. The rabbit was the only native who exhibited a civilized fear of man ; no doubt his prenatal impressions of the way in which man carries on his 'dominion' over animals have been kept vividly alive in his brain through the unceasing persecution of his youngsters and himself by the robber gulls ; the heaps of clean-picked rabbit - skeletons in all directions are striking evidence of their depredations, and gulls on watch at the rabbit-holes are a very common sight.

Our sociable 'ptarmigans' amused our men greatly by their innocent tameness, which at times led them into trouble. I was sitting one day with the gun across my knees, looking on at the skinning process, when a beautiful speci-men, which had been pottering round in search of blubber, actually jumped upon the gun-barrel, and began pecking gently at the brightly-polished sight. Whilst philosophizing on our moral right to kill off the poor elephants (such philosophy comes particularly cheap and easy after the event), my reverie was suddenly interrupted by a howl of rage from one of the foremen. On looking up, I saw a seal pike, the 'ptarmigan,' and a cloud of white feathers whirling through the air ; the explanation by Mr. Hasle was that the (let us say) blessed 'ptarmigan' had picked a hole in his beautiful *aelbatrost* egg, which was lying alongside of him.

Our 'ptarmigan' had not feathered legs like the Northern bird, which it otherwise so much resembled in appearance ; eggs appeared to be a delicacy to it. I also saw it feed on the soft and slippery moss uncovered along the shore at low water, unless it was in reality picking up marine insects from among the weeds. It was met with in numbers on the stony beach and on the cliffs near to the water, where it no doubt preferred to make its nest.

As if it was not enough to have discovered a flesh-eating 'ptarmigan,' our mate now fell in with numbers of 'gray geese,' which were stodging themselves with blubber to such an extent that they could not rise, and might be knocked on the head with a stick. The 'geese' turned out to be specimens of the gigantic petrel, and their difficulty in rising was explained by their heavy body and long wings necessitating a fair run before they

could get under way.   So ended our short dream
of roast goose.   This petrel or gull was present
in large numbers in Kerguelen ; its voracity was
extraordinary.

The varieties of penguins noticed during our
stay were the three described so many times
previously : the common and the crested penguin
(rock-hopper), and a larger kind with yellow stripes
on the cheeks, weighing about twenty pounds, and
therefore in size halfway between the common and
the king penguin.   Of the latter (the king penguin) only a few specimens were seen.

We came across a congregation of nearly
full-grown young penguins one day, with some
'elders' among them.   These latter undoubtedly
had a kind of military authority over the younger
ones, which at certain 'quack-quacks' would turn
to the right or left, and march along in rows like
well-trained soldiers, to the great amusement of
the onlookers.   The new coat of the full-fledged
youngsters is of a very handsome blue colour,
and their skins would surely be a magnificent
material for rugs, muffs, capes, etc.

The albatross nests in large numbers in Kerguelen ; we observed full-grown young birds, and
also fresh-laid eggs.   The latter make an excel-

lent dish; an omelette made with a single one of these enormous eggs afforded a respectable slice at supper to each of the four occupants of the cabin, all blessed with appetites of fine dimensions. Cormorants are also largely represented on our island.

The enterprising Messrs. Cook might do much worse than organize a tourist's expedition to Kerguelen in summer time for people who are tired of more common tracks. With good anchors the gales are ridden off in perfect safety, and the depth of the firths allows a steamer to penetrate into the very heart of the wild mountain ranges, which afford scenery of sublime grandeur. Much real exploration remains to be undertaken; fossil woods, coal-seams, petroleum-wells, etc., may be discovered during a summer's outing. The multitude of ducks and rabbits affords splendid sport. The climate, although raw and damp, is extremely bracing, and can have no terrors where a comfortable cabin awaits you on returning from the day's excursion.

*December* 27.—We got under steam at three o'clock in the morning, leaving the devastated Greenland Harbour, which is rather unsafe for vessels the draught of which does not allow them to penetrate to the head of the bay. With our 350 elephants on board, we steamed in fine, crisp weather and high good humour along the eastern shore, and turned into Royal Sound, the most noble and extensive of the Kerguelen harbours, filled with small islands, and affording a brilliant panorama on a clear day, with snow-clad mountains of 6,000 feet highest altitude to the west, and the imposing Crozier range to the north. Its twenty miles of land-locked water can shelter a numberless fleet against everything except the frequent hurricanes which blow down from the mountains.

On the shores were discovered flocks of elephants, and the boats, leaving at eight o'clock, returned about noon with full cargoes. The afternoon's hunt brought the day's bag up to 190 seals, whereupon we steamed further into the bay and anchored up for the night.

*December* 28.—During the night a layer of snow had fallen on the mountains, the pure whiteness giving to the landscape a new and charming effect. The catch is only ninety elephants this day, and we go further into the bay, anchoring up behind a large island, from whence the distance across the peninsula to Greenland Harbour is only a few miles.

*December 29 and 30.*—The days are spent in clearing up our decks after a fashion, boiling blubber, and shifting coals; the appearance of our ship is frightful, but nobody can think of appearances at present. What is worse, our salt begins to give out, which will soon prevent us from curing the skins; the boiling also is a very tedious proceeding, and we may have to carry the greater part of our blubber in its raw state.

*January* 1, 1894.—A magnificent day; warm sunshine, smiling landscape. In the afternoon a New Year's visit, very fatal to the elephants, was paid to a part of the shore where numbers of them had been noticed; about 100 were secured.

*January* 6.—No further sealing had been possible during the week. We had, however, found a particularly snug harbour behind an island, to which we returned for shelter at night. The bottom was clay of great holding power, and the water from a small stream ashore could be led straight into the boats. Clearing the blubber from the skins, boiling the former, emptying the tanks, etc., had kept everyone employed; besides this, we had on Thursday our second lesson in Kerguelen hurricanes, spending an anxious night, but holding our ground with both anchor-chains

5

out to their bitter end, and the propeller at work. Alas! the second warning is no more heeded than the first. Because, forsooth, an Arctic sealing hero, long deceased, would presumably not have lowered down the yards to the interruption of his sealing in regions where similar hurricanes in summer - time are unknown, we, the sons of Vikings, must uphold the supposed national honour under totally different conditions, and the safety of our vessel (the all-important object in my eyes) must be a secondary consideration, so long as the national vanity is appeased.

To-day (Saturday) the weather is again brilliant; calm and clear. I made use of the fine day to mount one of the neighbouring hills, from which a view of enchanting beauty was obtained—outwards, over islets and skerries to the open sea, to-day smiling in the sun and taking a fitful rest; inwards, over further islands and narrowing shores covered in green, with a background of blue mountain-ranges overtopped by snow-covered pinnacles. But for the pointed volcanic form of the latter, the landscape might well be that of a Norwegian fiord on a summer's day.

*January* 12.—We secured 133 elephants on the Monday (8th), and a few more during the next days; in all, 151. But a journey towards the inner end of the bay proved abortive; the seals appeared to have a predilection for the outer portions of the sound. During the day we had our third lesson in hurricanes, a lesson which took effect; the wind literally hurled itself down from the mountain-gorges against our apparently doomed vessel. The firth is too narrow to form waves of any considerable height; but the water was 'scooped up,' and whirled about like flying ashes, filling the air with a scud of spoondrift, whilst the mountain-sides appeared to be steaming or smoking. When the squall struck the vessel, she heeled over till the water poured in over the deck through the scuppers. One of our boats had been left towing behind; the line parted, and in a few minutes the boat was blown against the shore, forced out of the water, and turned over and over by the wind until a grass bank stopped its careering.

The chains were slacked out till the last fathom, and the engine kept working ahead continuously; but as even so the vessel showed signs of drifting, it was decided that the suitable moment had now arrived for lowering our topgallant and royal yards, and the poor boatswain was ordered aloft, whilst

we followed his perilous ascent in breathless suspense from the deck, his clothes fluttering madly
in the screeching gale.   By good luck he escaped
being blown into the water, and the yards came
safely down, the shade of the Arctic hero looking frowningly down on an effete generation.

The effect of the rigging-down was magical ;
the gale continued, but everyone felt that our
anchors were now more than equal to the strain.
The tardy snugging process was later on continued, and we rode off gale after gale in perfect
comfort ; why baring the topgallant masts should
have such an influence may be difficult to explain,
but the fact remains, that the vessel after the
rigging-down appeared like a new being.

I have at times felt that my readers may consider me too fond of superlatives in the descriptions of Southern gales ; but a perusal of sober
reports like those by Sir James Ross comforts me
by proving that even stronger language would be
justified.

The next days brought squall after squall, but no
further discomfort beyond preventing our hunting.

*January* 15.—Spent in vain search for elephants.
Although fish in large quantities must exist round
the islands to maintain the millions of sea-birds,

we were particularly unfortunate in our attempts to catch them. A single specimen was secured about twelve inches in length ; according to the Captain, it appeared related to the blennies, which the rocky nature of the sea-bottom made a likely guess.

The complete failure of our attempts at fishing in the Kerguelen firths, and later on at Campbell Islands, was a source of much surprise to us all ; I must confess that I had ascribed the similar failure on the part of previous expeditions to the supposed simplicity of the ordinary English sailor in respect of sea-fishing ; my national vanity was therefore much humbled by finding that even our most cunning wiles and most tempting baits were of no avail. At the time we liked to ascribe this apathy on the part of Southern fish to their state of heathen ignorance of the blessings of civilization, and their general want of education ; but in the late Professor Moseley's treatise on the *Challenger* Expedition I have later on found a beautifully simple explanation of the at first puzzling anomaly-islands with bays practically devoid of fish, whilst the surrounding seas are teeming with them, as is proved by the contents of the stomachs of penguins and other marine birds. Professor Moseley points out that the myriads of birds living and feeding undisturbed on and around these Southern islands must of necessity practically exterminate all fish life in the immediate vicinity of their nurseries ; the extraordinary diving powers of the penguins will further carry this extermination to very considerable depths.

The same authority rather upsets my deduction, that the extreme tameness of the *chionis* (sheathbills) proves a long absence from Kerguelen of resident sealing-parties. He proves that centuries of contact with man alone suffice to teach wild animals the true nature of his ' dominion ' over them. The wild geese passing over Europe have had the advantage of such prolonged contact, and are in consequence the wariest birds living. The wild goose of the Falkland Islands has only been schooled for a couple of centuries, and can still be knocked down with a stick. Many centuries must evidently pass before the brain of our beautiful *chionis* acquires the prenatal impressions which will cause it to instinctively shun the human visitor, with his generally evil designs on its feathers or flesh.

The instinctive terror of man evinced by the

Kerguelen rabbits—descendants of European and civilized forbears — proves the correctness of Professor Moseley's theory in a different way ; just as the knowledge of man's real nature is a matter of extremely slow growth, the lesson once taught is so well remembered that it survives the time of active danger, and remains in the animal brain as a never-slumbering instinct.

*January* 16.—Weather being fine, we steamed across to the exposed east shore, where 108 seals were captured and brought into the boats with infinite labour on account of the surf, which compelled the men to carry the skins to the boats through water reaching to their waists.

On my return from a neighbouring hilltop, I came across a single elephant at a marvellous distance from, and height above, the shore, considering his difficulty of locomotion.

He was a misogynist, undoubtedly, holding views insulting to my better-half, and the fair sex in general ; why should he live, then, when his brother must die, who has come thousands of miles, and abjured eating for months, in order to pay his court to fifteen hundredweight and more of pining beauty that awaits him with the former season's love-pledge ? Urged on by these calculations of justice, and of his great value in the form of oil, I coaxed him down to the shore, with a rest from time to time, as misogyny and asthma appeared to go together. To convert a misogynist into a good family man is impossible; let us, then, attempt only what is possible, and convert him into good machinery oil and strong leather.

Seriously, however, I would soon gladly have restored my philosopher to his hilltop, had it been possible. The moral discomfort of living by killing is never more acutely felt than after a personal interview, so to speak, with an individual member of the species which you hesitate little to slaughter by the herd.

*January* 17.—We had returned for the night to our usual anchorage. The day broke with fine weather, and 120 elephants were secured towards the mouth of the bay on one of our first hunting-fields. Returning late at night to our usual place for the night, we touched the ground, but fortunately had sufficient impetus to go right over the shoal.

*January* 19.—Yesterday was spent in clearing our decks again. To-day we try the eastern coast once more; but few animals are left, and the great surf makes the work of landing and shipping skins both laborious and dangerous.

Our total capture is now 1,280 seals—*i.e.*, about 800 casks of oil, the value being roughly £1,600, without counting the skins. Our outfit is there fore already more than paid for ; but full cargo would be more acceptable still, and we decide to explore further bays. The voyage south must be put off till another season, as the summer is already on the wane. Our supply of many necessary articles of food begins to give out, and the leakage of our heavy vessel has increased to such an extent that a stoppage of three hours in the pumping is enough for the water to reach the lower level of our boiler.

We unfortunately did not penetrate to the parts of the island where Sir James made his wonderful discoveries of huge fossilized trees, and the other evidences of a Kerguelen covered with luxuriant forests and vegetation before volcanic and other disturbances reduced it to its present state of sombre but withal imposing desolation. Neither did we see the active volcano reported as existing on one part of the coast.

*January* 23.—A visit yesterday towards Shoal Water Bay was fruitless ; this bay was literally filled with marine growth, and difficult of access. The original field round Greenland Bay brought us 120 more elephants. Snow at night, a low thermometer, and plenty of wind, reminded us that the autumn was now drawing near. The frequent gales interrupted the sealing badly, as we dared not go far away except when the barometer looked reasonable, and we always returned at night to one of our tried anchorages.

*January* 27.—We yesterday steamed along the lofty forbidding shore westwards to Swain's Bay against a high sea, and ran into the firth between towering mountains, with no foreshore, and consequently no seals. To-day we ran into a bay so narrow as hardly to afford room for turning the vessel. Our catch here was about 100 seals the first day, and a few more some days later ; but the high wind and violent surf gave us much trouble and some anxiety—one of the loaded boats could be forced against the sea only by our slacking out another boat from the vessel with a rope, and heaving the two alongside with the steam-winch.

But our greed must not lead us into folly, and the departure for Melbourne must not be further delayed. Our leak is increasing ; hardly a day passes but we are told by the steward that some necessary or other is either entirely gone or rapidly vanishing. Of flour we have none ; the sugar will be a delight of the past in a week or two ; the butter can be drawn out for another four weeks at most ; by mixing the coffee with plenty of browned peas (an adulteration which does not appreciably affect the taste or colour), it may be spun out for the same period.

The next days were therefore spent in completing the boiling of blubber, salting skins, filling water, cleaning our boiler, rigging up yards, fastening the boats, and the thousand other tasks coming under the heading of preparing for sea.

On February 3 we steamed out from our safe anchorage for the last time, and soon drew away from the outwardly inhospitable island, which had brought us in a few weeks a cargo that we at the time estimated at a value of £3,000. As the instigator and promoter of the expedition, and in a measure responsible for its commercial success or failure, I could not see the Kerguelen peaks disappear without a feeling of attachment towards the rugged, desolate land, and of thankfulness to Providence, which had so bountifully rewarded our first effort.

The next week brought us a succession of fine days, with gentle breezes and warm sunshine. As the engine had to be kept going steadily, and our coals were getting very low indeed, we were actually pining a little for the boisterous gale which we had just left behind.

The work of our engine so far has been as follows :

(Nine barrels of coal = one ton.)

$\frac{1}{1}$ speed during 91 watches × 5 barrels = 455 barrels.
$\frac{3}{4}$    ,,    ,,    66    ,,    × 4  ,,    = 264   ,,
$\frac{1}{2}$    ,,    ,,    96    ,,    × 3  ,,    = 288   ,,
Slow   ,,    ,,    55    ,,    × 2  ,,    = 110   ,,

         Total consumption by engine    1,117  ,,

Pumping    ... 248 watches × 1$\frac{1}{4}$ barrels = 310 barrels
Blubber-boiling 40    ,,    × 5    ,,    = 200  ,,
Galley ...    ... 125 days    × 1    ,,    = 125  ,,
Present quantity in bunkers    ...    ... about 420  ,,

            Total ...     ...     2,172  ,,

Bought at Christiania ...     ... 200 tons.
   ,,     Las Palmas ...     ... 41  ,,

            Total ...     ...    241  ,,

241 tons at 9 barrels per ton = 2,169 barrels.

The fine weather allowed us to begin a task exceedingly urgent, viz., the cleaning of our ship in general, and our deck in particular. During the hard work at Kerguelen the deck, railing, etc., had got into a frightful state of filth—oil, blubber, soot, blood everywhere in a heavy layer, which only yielded to warm water and soda applied with lots of elbow-grease. After awhile the patches of clean deck began to widen and run together, and masts, railings, boats, etc., in turn received our attention, whilst the engineer swung about aloft painting his funnel and brightening his whistle. By the time that ‚stronger and more favourable winds had carried us uneventfully within sight of the friendly Australian shore, we were again presentable.

We anchored up on February 23 off Williamstown to discharge powder, explosive shells, etc., and soon found our cabin full of the many good friends and acquaintances who had assisted me so nobly in my Australian efforts, and followed our Norwegian enterprise with intense interest : Mr. Trapp ; our Consul ; Baron von Mueller ; Messrs. Potter and Griffiths, of the Geographical Society, etc. — everybody enthusiastic and congratulatory at the auspicious beginning of our expedition.

It was Saturday, and I therefore hurried ashore as soon as hospitality permitted, despatching to our veteran at home the telegram which I had so often indited since leaving Kerguelen :

'Safely ; 1,600 seals, 95 tons blubber, part boiled.'

Shall I be able to despatch an even more satisfactory telegram when I return from the mysterious South Victoria Land ? I hope for the best, and in the meantime all the anxiety and worry of the last half-year are forgotten in the hospitality and friendship tendered to me by my Australian acquaintances, and the general interest and good feeling shown towards us in the colony.

---

NOTE.—In my short description of the most characteristic of the Kerguelen birds, I have omitted the reference due to the elegant little terns, which by their jerky flight and magnificently red-coloured legs introduce a more homely feature into the otherwise outlandish bird-life. Their backs and wings are darker than in the Northern species, and their number is much smaller than in Northern latitudes; around Iceland, for instance, the sea is at times covered for a mile or more with a dense crowd of these graceful birds.

# CHAPTER VI.

### MELBOURNE.—INTERMEDIATE VOYAGE.

DURING our run from Kerguelen, I had suddenly
been asked the question, Who are really the
owners of these islands? Well, who are they?
Frenchmen, Englishmen, or Australians? What
an ending to our hopes if we find, on arriving at
Melbourne, that our hard-won cargo is to be
confiscated, and the crew imprisoned as buccaneers,
pirates, or at least as common poachers!

The idea gave rise to many uncomfortable
reflections; but week after week passed in Melbourne, and nobody seemed to feel injured,
neither has any claim to this day been made
against us for trespass.

The first weeks were a time of extreme activity
for me. The cargo had to be disposed of, and
the ship's business attended to, our vessel docked
in preparation for her intermediate whaling trip,

and the kind hospitality of the town accepted, so far as time would allow.

The colonial enthusiasm for our expedition, as representing the first serious attempt to explore and exploit Antarctic waters commercially, was an agreeable surprise to us, as we had been afraid that our nationality might have given rise to a somewhat natural jealousy. As a matter of fact, we saw no evidence whatever of any such feeling, whilst the scientific bodies of Australia were also earnestly anxious to assist, and enable us to forward our commercial aims, as well as to collect useful scientific data during our prospective voyage.

A social reception was arranged in our honour at the Royal Society's rooms, at the invitation of the Geographical Society, the Antarctic Exploration Committee, and the Royal Society, Professor Kernot presiding.

In the speeches the members of the expedition were not forgotten, whilst Baron von Mueller proposed the health of Commander Foyn, but for whose generosity the expedition could not have been carried out.

I then read a paper which I had written, explaining the purposes of the projected expedition, and the possibilities of Antarctic waters in respect of whaling and sealing, after which I tried to return the compliment paid to us, by inviting the company present to an *al-fresco* entertainment on board the *Antarctic*. The ship was cleared and beautified as far as possible for the occasion, the digesters (try-works), whaling gear, etc., were inspected with much interest, and finally a gun, with harpoon and line, was fired in order to thrill the visitors.

The blubber realized 95 tons of oil, which I disposed of in Melbourne for about £1,775. In sanguine moments we had estimated the value of the skins at several pounds apiece, or at least £1 each as the most sober minimum. Their enormous dimensions seemed to justify our anticipations. Many of them measured nearly 100 square feet in area, and their thickness (about half an inch) allowed of their being 'split' into a number of layers, by the all too-cunning machinery at the disposal of modern tanners. The apparent similarity of the sea-elephant's hide to that of the walrus was another factor which added to the value of his hide in our estimation.

But here a severe disappointment was in store for us. The first colonial offers were scornfully

6

rejected, although we should have realized very nearly the above minimum price by accepting them.

As time went on, however, the inferior quality of the hides became distressingly apparent. The animals were undoubtedly out of sorts at the time of our visit : the hairs were moulting, and the skins themselves of little strength ; in many cases they also exhibited hairless, scurvy patches. As a matter of fact, the breeding season of the elephants was long past at the time of our visit, and the animals we found had landed for the season's renewal of their hairs, a time when the skin itself is necessarily affected by their distemper.

A pair of shoes made from a piece of tanned hide felt and looked perfection, but after only a fortnight's wear dissolution of sole and uppers set in so rapidly that an early and discreet funeral became necessary. My great pride and boasting at their début led to many embarrassing inquiries on their sudden disappearance.

Ultimately the skins were consigned to London, where they realized a paltry £200, the greater part of which disappeared in the form of expenses and freight. Still, I feel sure that a much higher price could have been obtained had we managed to find the best market, as the demand for real hide, even though inferior, is almost inexhaustible in connection with the manufacture of shoes and trunks, sold as ' Best Quality !'

When captured at the proper seasons, I understand that the sea-elephant yields a hide of considerable value, and a London authority informs me that our cargo of skins even in its bad state should have realized about £1 per hide—that is, unless they had been utterly spoilt or rotted in transit—a thing which did not happen, as far as we know.

Before leaving the commercial review of our voyage up to this date, I must, in justice to myself, refer briefly to a matter which I know to be of little interest to the general public.

The man of honour who, by his representations of reasonable prospect of gain, has caused other people to embark a large capital in any venture, can have little peace of mind, unless a favourable result is either attained, or prevented only by accidents beyond human foresight or control.

Mr. Foyn had increased my personal responsibility by repeatedly stating—during initial difficulties in the fitting out, with which I have not troubled the reader—that he would never go through with the venture but for my sake, and his original offer to me.

When, therefore, my business friends in Melbourne, excited with our early success, proposed to buy out Mr. Foyn, and continue the work at their own risk, it was with a feeling of great satisfaction that I wired to Norway for the price at which Mr. Foyn would transfer the vessel and outfit to a colonial company.

The sum demanded — £10,000 — was nearly twice the amount contemplated by my friends, who accordingly drew back. It transpired later on that Mr. Foyn had meant to include in his price the cargo, which at the time was valued at £3,000. Even so, the figure asked for would have been difficult, not to say impossible, to obtain ; but I had the moral satisfaction of knowing that an opportunity had been given my veteran friend of retiring with honour, and even with some profit, from a venture the speculative nature of which I had never tried to hide, and which must, in fact, have been apparent to any thinking man, much more to one so experienced as Mr. Foyn.

On docking the *Antarctic*, the ridiculously trivial cause of her leakage was soon discovered.

The blow-off pipe had rusted away close to the skin of the vessel, and therefore out of sight, leaving a hole so large that a jelly-fish, amongst other things, had been sucked through it and forced in amongst the ship's timbers. A few pounds were enough to repair this matter, which had caused us all such great and constant anxiety during our voyage to Australia.

As a good deal of innocent, and some unfriendly, criticism has been directed against the promoters of the expedition, in connection with the supposed craziness of our good ship, I must be permitted to enlighten those who have no personal knowledge of sealing vessels on the point. The leak itself was not observed as at all serious before we left Norway. To imagine that Commander Foyn would have allowed us to depart on a particularly perilous journey without locating and stopping a palpable and serious leak is an insult to the memory of this great man. That I myself, a benedict with a large family, and with a whole-some respect for the dangers of the deep, should have willingly entrusted my life to the chances of a sinking ship is also difficult to imagine. Nor-wegian sealing vessels are, on the other hand, built with such tremendous massiveness of timbers

and planking that they are as strong at the end
of twenty-five years as on the day they took the
water.   Our vessel was too small to be profitable
in Arctic sealing, where the whole chance of profit
or loss is decided by a single brief annual cruise ;
but in all other respects—barring the accidental leak
—no sailor who had spent a few months on board
our ship could avoid admiring and loving her for
her sterling qualities in the way of seaworthiness,
strength, and sailing powers.   The smallness of
our vessel would have prevented us from making
a large fortune, had we fallen in with unlimited
numbers of seals or Right whales ; but for our
immediate mission—that of exploration, of spying
out the land, or the sea, rather, and of pioneering
more ambitious ventures—the *Antarctic* was in all
respects an admirably suitable vessel.

With a few more trifling repairs, and a thorough
overhaul and replenishing of provisions, the
*Antarctic* was ready for her winter cruise in
search of Right and sperm whales round Campbell
and neighbouring islands.   Before describing,
however, the events of this intermediate voyage,
I will relate in sequence our exciting experiments
in gunnery and explosive bombs, although part of
this comedy really was enacted at a later period.

Our experience with steam - whalers in the
Arctic seas had taught us the importance of
harpooning and killing the whales, if possible,
from the vessel itself, thus permitting of a rapidity
and range in pursuit, especially in the case of a
school of whales, unattainable where the actual
capture is effected by small boats propelled with
oars and bad language at a time when speed,
order, and serenity of mind are all-important.
But how could we prevent the powerful animals
from snapping the line as it becomes taut, and
before the inertia of our heavy vessel is overcome?
Experience has proved that no rope of a practic-
able size will hold at this critical moment where
the animal harpooned is of any weight.

A single expedient evidently remained. The
wound or wounds inflicted on the whale by the
first attack from the vessel must be so terrible as
to kill it on the spot, or at least deprive it of the
greater part of its strength. When firing a single
gun with harpoon and explosive shell, it is a mere
fluke if the latter explodes so near to a vital part
as to kill the whale immediately. The following
scheme was therefore evolved by the collective
wisdom of the members of our expedition : The
attack should be made with two guns fired

simultaneously, the one carrying the usual harpoon with shell and line, the other throwing a heavy bomb with a powerful bursting charge, and a propelling charge so adjusted as to drive the bomb halfway through the whale, at which point it was to explode, freeing the soul of our poor sea-rover from his carnal prison, to which we were to hold on by the harpoon and line.

The beauty of this plan (on paper) is easily observed—adjust your fuse to explode the bomb within a second or two of firing your gun, arrange your propelling charge so that the bomb shall not go right through the animal, hit the whale, and there you are!

Full of self-satisfaction, we hastened to put our plan to the test. A workman attached to the arsenal made the fuses to our design, and we tried the bombs against a sand-hill outside the harbour. The fuse—our masterpiece—depended for its action on the progress of combustion of a fine thread of gunpowder communicating between the propelling and bursting charges. The gun is loaded and directed against the hill amid breath-less suspense. As the trigger is pulled we turn towards the sand-hill to watch the effect of the exploding shell. Click! goes the trigger, but instead of the expected mild explosion to follow comes a tremendous confused roar, and a scattering and pattering far and wide of fragments of iron. The bomb has burst in the gun. It must, of course, be an accident, as the length of powder-thread allowed should delay the explosion of the bursting charge by a perfectly definite interval of time. Let us try once more. The cannon is reloaded with less serenity, and fired with greater discretion. The result is the same—a tremendous bang and a quantity of soaring iron.

What is the explanation? After much cogitation, it is suggested, and proved by a practical test, either that the rate of combustion of a confined powder-thread varies greatly with the accompanying pressure, or that the thread is blown bodily into the bursting charge, so firing it prematurely. These little facts are no doubt well known to artillerists; we had to rediscover them for ourselves.

By reducing the section of the channel in the fuses, and making it less direct, we successively arrived at bombs which would explode at the muzzle, close by the muzzle, and finally more or less at the desired distance. But throughout our voyage the beautiful uncertainty and capriciousness of our home-made bombs lent a particular excitement to their use.

When tried in actual whaling, our scheme proved an unqualified failure. Still, I cannot admit any inherent lack of value or practicability ; but gun discipline and drill were not pursued with sufficient seriousness on board our vessel, and the consequence was a series of burlesque performances whenever we had a fair chance of killing a whale from the vessel. Either the harpoon gun alone was fired and the bomb gun forgotten, or *vice-versâ ;* at other times one or other of the guns was not ready for firing, the caps were forgotten, etc. For the reasons given in a previous chapter, describing the methods adopted in Norway for the killing of blue whales, the chances of successful capture must always be small where the harpoon is fired from a heavy ship, and not from a small and specially equipped steamer. The chances must be smaller still, unless the explosive shells are absolutely dependable, and the crew have considerable practice and are steadily drilled.

Whilst I remained behind to complete the disposal of our cargo and prepare for the supreme effort—the voyage South—the *Antarctic* left

Melbourne on April 12, 1894, to try her luck at whaling in the winter months.

I saw her leave with considerable misgiving. I have already referred to the fact that the Captain and the writer occupied a somewhat anomalous position towards each other, a position which could only be rendered tolerable by mutual consideration. As the manager abroad I had great powers, but did not feel that they justified me in interfering in the actual direction of what any capable skipper would justly consider his domain. My scrupulous observance of this self-imposed restriction did not, in my opinion, meet with similar consideration on the part of the Captain.

On the present occasion I advised that two of our short, heavy, unwieldy Norwegian boats should be replaced, before the start from Melbourne, by two of the long, light, easily handled boats used in actual Right and sperm whaling. No, the proposal was insulting; we were to show the Australians how Norwegian sailors did their whaling with Norwegian boats. We did show them, but the exhibition was not edifying.

With the Kerguelen gales fresh in memory I also offered to buy or hire for the cruise two heavy anchors and an extra strong chain cable, but was told by the Captain that this would be needless waste.

In the face of his opinion, I did not feel justified in insisting that boats, anchors, and chain should be bought.

A plan of the cruise to be made had been laid down in Melbourne. Three weeks were first to be spent around certain parts of Tasmania. As the whales did not turn up at once, and the weather looked threatening, only a few days were spent in this region, and the *Antarctic* laid her course for Campbell Islands just as the old sailing whaler stationed at Hobart Town stood out of harbour to look for fish.

The next tidings I received of the vessel were contained in a telegram from New Zealand, signed by Mr. Hatch, the owner of a small vessel, the *Gratitude :*

'*Antarctic* left wrecked at Campbell, having struck Terror Shoal. Main mast sprung, loss of anchor, etc., requiring seventy tons of coals and immediate assistance.'

My feelings on receiving the news of this terrible blow can be imagined, but the most bewildering part was the absence of direct news from the vessel. The *Gratitude* must have arrived with the report, otherwise Mr. Hatch could not telegraph as he did. Why was no confirmatory statement telegraphed me from the Captain or officers of the *Antarctic*?

I could only conclude that the wire from Mr. Hatch was sent in accordance with instructions given by Captain Kristensen to the skipper of the *Gratitude*. IMMEDIATE assistance is asked for, and without it the vessel may become a total wreck. Mr. Hatch offered in his telegram to send his vessel back to Campbell Islands with the anchor, coals, etc., and under the circumstances I felt it my duty to close with him on the best possible terms : hard terms, certainly, but not violently exorbitant, considering the urgency of the case, and the merciless way in which mariners are usually and legally permitted to benefit when rendering assistance to unfortunate brethren—a survival, no doubt, from the customs in vogue centuries ago in cases of shipwreck.

Eight days afterwards, when the *Gratitude* had already left for Campbell, a LETTER, sent in the ordinary way by post from Bluff, arrived from Captain Kristensen, describing the accident, and asking for an anchor and forty tons of coal to be sent him ; but bad as was his plight, there was no such urgency and peril as described by Mr. Hatch, and a large amount of money would have been saved if the *Gratitude* had brought a written message to be telegraphed to me, or if one of the mates had been sent with her to New Zealand.

In describing shortly the melancholy voyage of the *Antarctic* to Campbell Islands, I will follow closely the printed narrative by Captain Kristensen, to make sure that no injustice to this gentleman shall be rendered by the strong personal views which I must always retain as to his conduct of the short cruise which marks the commencing decline of our lucky star henceforth.

During the first days after leaving Tasmania a violent hurricane was blowing, which the good vessel rode off in her usual manner.

On May 1 Auckland was sighted, the islands which were granted to Messrs. Enderby as a whaling station in the days of Sir James Ross.

No Right whales could be seen, however, during the stay here ; the great numbers of fur-seals had to be left alone owing to the close season, which is enforced by the New Zealand Government in these regions.

The vessel proceeded to Campbell Islands, which were sighted on May 14, the wind increasing to half a gale, with tremendous squalls, as the land drew near and darkness began to fall.

Nevertheless the Captain tried to enter North-East Harbour, but the squalls blew so violently down the valley—as they always do in the islands in these latitudes—that no advance was possible, whilst the danger of drifting down upon the outlying rocks was considerable, with the ship not answering her helm.

In spite of this lesson and rebuff, the *Antarctic* was kept going, close along the unknown shore towards Perseverance Harbour, the mouth of which was safely reached.

By forcing the boiler the vessel was made to slowly advance between the squalls into the firth, but in the darkness it was impossible to make out the exact bearings, and the vessel grounded on Terror Shoal.

She was got off with much labour after the fore topsail had been set, but as the sail immediately after was blown to shreds, the vessel again got unmanageable, and the anchors had to be dropped in the middle of the harbour in twenty fathoms of water.

The Captain's explanation of his reason for trying to make an unknown and uninhabited harbour at night, in the teeth of a gale, was that otherwise he might never have arrived at Campbell that winter, possibly even have drifted round Cape Horn!

Much worse than the grounding was, however, to follow. The gale continued with heavy squalls throughout the 17th and the 18th; but in spite of the Kerguelen lesson no attempts were made to lower yards or snug the vessel. As the rigging-down was next day actually carried out when the hurricane was at its very highest, but too late to save the vessel from shipwreck, it cannot be argued that the gale prevented the operation. In spite of a third anchor attached to the strongest cable on board being dropped, the vessel began at midnight on the 18th to drift right out of the harbour, before the cyclonic gusts which invariably accompany heavy gales on islands in these latitudes, although they do not reach any great distance away from the shores.

The idea was now to buoy and let go the anchor-chains, and make for the open sea, where the vessel would be safe. But before this could be effected the cable broke, and the wind shifted to south-west, with cyclonic gusts driving the vessel close under the precipitous mountain-walls. Nothing remained but to cut down the mainmast and rig down the yards on the fore-mast, after which drastic snugging-down process the anchors held, and the poor wreck of a ship was kept swinging before the squall less than her own length from the mountain-side.

On the 19th the vessel could steam further into the harbour, into more sheltered water, and during the next days most of the rigging was saved and got on board, whilst also the first Right whale was seen.

On the 31st the rigging up of jury-mast, etc., was so far completed that the vessel could leave Perseverance Harbour in search of Right whales, of which two were sighted and pursued in vain, our boats proving lamentably heavy and clumsy. Spending the night in North East Harbour, the vessel again steamed out next morning, several whales being pursued by four of the boats, but without result, for the same reason as on the previous day.

Heaving up the anchors next morning, it was

7

found that the best one had been lost; the cause
of this disaster I do not know to this day.

The day was lost in vain attempts to recover
the vanished anchor; a wire hawser was made
fast ashore, the other end buoyed, and the vessel
later on kept riding to the one remaining anchor
and this hawser.

The next days were spent in vain dredging for
the anchor and looking for whales, which were
frequently chased, without the boats being able
to get within striking distance. The time was
now considered to have arrived for rectifying the
unpardonable mistake of not obtaining suitable
boats before the departure, and a light boat was
lengthened to afford room for more rowers.

On the 9th a whale rose so close to the
Captain's boat that it could nearly be touched
with the hand, but on trying to harpoon it the
cap did not explode, and before it could be exchanged for another, a second boat had fired its
harpoon without hitting in a vital part; the line
got mixed up with floating kelp and broke, thus
ending the day's fishing.

On June 12 two Right whales were seen, but
the seas and the current were too serious to allow
of pursuit. The same day a small New Zealand

vessel, the *Gratitude* already referred to, called at the island, having fetched five sealers from Macquarie Islands, who had 'tried out' 120 tons of oil during the summer, twenty tons only from elephant blubber, the rest from penguins.

The Captain, Mr. Brown, explained that he suffered great hardships during his voyages to Macquarie Islands to fetch the men who stayed there, sometimes for two years, collecting and boiling blubber. He could anchor under the lee of the shore in a westerly wind, but could only land in good weather, on account of the tremendous surf. If an easterly gale sprang up, it was necessary to buoy the anchors and haul off, returning when the weather moderated, everything having to be floated or rafted to and from the shore.

When the *Gratitude* left for New Zealand a letter was given to the skipper to be posted to me from the nearest place of call, but no written message for telegraphic transmission was handed him, a neglect the consequence of which has already been explained.

To return to our hapless vessel. The next weeks were spent in the same tragi-comical attempts at whaling. Many animals were sighted, but as a rule pursued in vain.

*June* 23.—Four boats pursuing a Right whale, one of them succeeded in harpooning, and stuck to the animal for two and a half hours, when the line caught round a rock and parted.

*June* 27.—Intervening days too stormy to allow of hunting. Several whales observed this day. One of them, harpooned from the mate's boat, rushed into the breakers to free itself, preventing the boats from approaching closely. Darkness falling and the wind increasing, it became necessary to cut the line and let the animal go, representing a lost value of £500 to £700.

*June* 28.—Many whales sighted (all the whales met with at Campbell were Right whales), some of them 'fishing' in the tide eddies with the tail high above the water.

At 10 a.m. one of the boats harpooned a whale, which a comrade apparently tried to assist, rolling over and over with it as often as it came to the surface. During the whole day no mortal wound could be inflicted; the ship's guns proved of little use; this animal also took refuge among the breakers, and the firing of loose harpoons, as well as lancing, failed to dislodge it. Two of the boats remained with the whale until past midnight, when the increasing wind and sea nearly swamped

them, and the dying animal had to be cut adrift
with much heartburning.

*June* 29.—Whales in pairs and large schools
are sighted ; all boats away in chase until a fish
was at last fixed towards the evening, the harpoon
going right through its body close to the tail ; a
shot from the vessel severed the line, but another
harpoon was fired before the animal got away,
and after a tremendous cannonade from the ship
and all the boats, the first and last 'kill' on the
voyage was brought about.

Few whales were sighted after this date, and
none could be manœuvred within striking distance ; the vessel was therefore headed for Auckland, where no Right whales could be found, but
where the *Gratitude* overtook our ship and delivered the two anchors and seventy tons of coals.

A few days spent cruising round Solander
Islands were also fruitless as regards whaling.
The voyage was continued along the coast of
New Zealand, and several aimless and useless
visits paid to various harbours.

The enormous waste of time at Campbell in
shipwreck, rigging-up and repairs, dredging for
the lost anchor, vain rowing after whales, etc.,
and the useless visits referred to, had shortened

the whaling season to such an extent that little
time remained for a trip to Kermadee Islands,
where plenty of 'fish' are caught in winter-time
by sailing-vessels, and where steam-power should
have told heavily in our favour.  The *Antarctic*
was therefore once more headed for Melbourne,
where I had been anxiously awaiting news from
her.

It is difficult to know whether I should laugh
or cry on reading the Captain's story of the
voyage : when the vessel is wrecked under his
leadership, and the seas to which I have directed
him are swarming with Right whales, which he
cannot reach on account of his own mistakes,
this is the moment which he thinks suitable for
an attack on the sanguine manager, 'who knows
little about whaling, either in Southern or any
other waters.'

How different was the second entry of our poor
vessel into Melbourne Harbour on August 21
compared with the first triumphal arrival only
six months previously !  Then every heart was
full of elation and thankfulness for the past, hope
for the future, and gratification at the universal
sympathy from all around us, whilst our deep-
laden ship, with her new paint and gay colours,

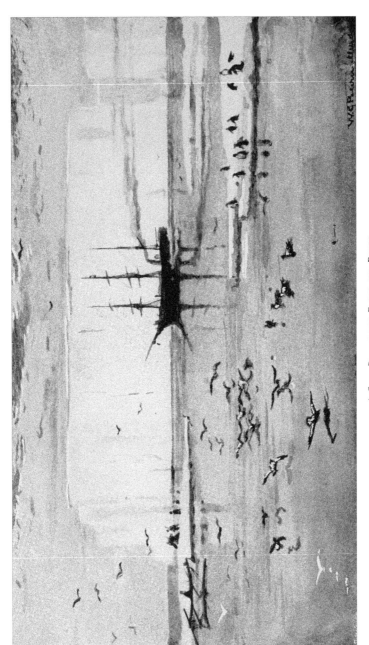

A Calm Day among Floes and Bergs.

bore outward testimony to our success. Now our vessel steams in bearing signs of defeat and failure in her patched-up mast and generally crippled appearance, every heart oppressed with sullen gloom, born of the feeling that the defeat was undeserved, the failure not due to the unavoidable accidents which we accept with fortitude and a 'better luck next time.'

The many accidents and failures in the whale-hunt at Campbell Islands were explained and accounted for in various ways by the different members of the expedition; but all the accounts agreed on one point—that there was no lack of Right whales round the islands during the visit there of the *Antarctic*.

In part explanation and part justification of the poor result of the whaling should be mentioned our defective shells, which not only were erratic as regards bursting, but also frequently did not penetrate sufficiently into the whale attacked. We were entirely unprepared for this difficulty, viz., want of penetrative power, as our experience from Arctic waters gave us no warning in this respect, and I cannot even now explain the reason satisfactorily, as our shells were fired from a cannon with a driving charge which was increased until the gun supports in some cases carried away, whilst on the other hand propelling charges of the shells generally used by Southern whalers are so small as to allow firing from the shoulder with a kind of heavy blunderbuss.

Many of our harpoons also did not penetrate fairly through the blubber into the flesh of the whales, although the driving charges were increased until the firing became distinctly dangerous. As the Southern whaler flings his harpoon by hand, this lack of penetration on the part of our harpoons was still more puzzling.

In the interval before our next voyage these defects in our shells and harpoons were remedied to the best of our power. Two excellent whaling-boats were also procured, and so the mistake rectified which during the last cruise had cost us more dearly than all the other shortcomings combined.

The solitary whale captured at Campbell realized six tons of oil, disposed of in Melbourne, and three hundredweights of whalebone, which I consigned to London for sale.

\*    \*    \*    \*    \*

The repairs of damage suffered at Campbell, new main mast and rigging, etc., swallowed up the profits remaining from our last voyage.

Replenishing our stores, provisioning for nine months, and the general overhaul before we could safely start on our great voyage, ran into considerable figures ; with the repairs mentioned, the total was nearly £2,000.

During my last months in Australia, great enthusiasm for our enterprise, and anxiety to assist me in every way, were evinced from all quarters. The military authorities suggested the loan of a Nordenfeldt gun with which to pepper the schools of Right whales described by Sir James Ross ; the Geographical Society assisted me by the loan of charts and books, offered us the loan of instruments, and at one time contemplated sending with us one or more young men of science. The memory of the overflowing kindness and appreciation shown towards the expedition and myself by high and low in Melbourne will always constitute a real reward for my works, of which no man can rob me in the future.

One of the most interesting of my new acquaintances was Dr. J. J. Wild, of *Challenger* renown ; he brought me one day a number of his sketches and charts from Kerguelen, and his enthusiastic interest for this snow-capped and sombre, but romantic and grandiose island is still so great that he will undoubtedly be one of the first passengers to subscribe his name, should the suggested Cook's tourist trip come off in a near future.

The celebrated Arctic explorer, recently killed by a regrettable accident, Mr. Eivind Astrup (Lieutenant Peary's companion on his Greenland journeys) had asked and obtained Mr. Foyn's permission to accompany us on the trip to South Victoria Land. Mr. William S. Bruce, the Scotch naturalist who accompanied the *Balæna* on her expedition to the south of Cape Horn, had likewise sought and obtained leave to go with us. I had looked forward to their company with keen delight, as I confess to a liking for congenial society. Unfortunately these two gentlemen could not reach Melbourne in time for our early start, and I had already resigned myself to the prospect of the old solitary life on board, when Mr. Carsten Egeberg Borchgrevinck one fine day called on me, informing me that he was a student from Christiania University, highly connected through his relations, and extremely anxious to join our expedition. His family was known to me in a general way, and the prospect of a real companion was so cheering that I promised to do my best for him. The Captain, to commence with, would not hear of it, with the universal and pardonable objection of skippers to carrying 'passengers' on board a trading-vessel. Ultimately, however, he gave in to my representations, and allowed Mr. Borchgrevinck to sign on as a 'generally useful hand,' with his berth in the forecastle. Had the Prince of Wales desired a berth on our voyage, we could only have got him one by clearing either the Captain, the mates, or the writer out of the cabin. It is true that we had intended to build an extra cabin for the explorers above referred to, and for the colonial men of science who at one time contemplated joining us, but the qualifications and letters of introduction brought by Mr. Borchgrevinck were not such as to warrant a serious outlay in building extra cabins for him.

With the sole exception of my not giving my narrow crib up to Mr. Borchgrevinck and sleeping in the forecastle myself, I do not know of anything in reason which I omitted to do to increase the comfort of Mr. Borchgrevinck on board, and show my friendship for him. During the first two months following his arrival, he did the ship's work as far as it was requested of him.

After these two months he was allowed to employ the whole of his time practically as he pleased. He gave up his watches; took his meals with us in the cabin; occupied our rooms in the daytime; painted, sketched, stuffed birds, and studied my library of books relating to Antarctic exploration, of which he was utterly ignorant on joining; and altogether he occupied a position of ease, leisure, and freedom from anxiety and responsibility, unparalleled by that of anyone else on board. The companionship of this gentleman gave me great pleasure during our preparations for the voyage and during the voyage itself. I introduced him to my friends; at a later stage, I wrote him up in the papers, at his request; as he came on board without a full outfit, I gave him the blankets of my bed; and I supplied him with the very books and papers on which his notes were made, all with the greatest pleasure. But for certain subsequent events, I should be ashamed to enumerate the various ways in which I tried to show Mr. Borchgrevinck the regard due to one gentleman from another.

# CHAPTER VII.

*START FOR THE ANTARCTIC.—CAMPBELL ISLANDS.—*
*THE FIRST REBUFF.*

On September 26, 1894, we let go the last hawser connecting us with the friendly Australian shore, on which so much kindness had fallen to our lot, and steamed away from Melbourne Wharf amid hurrahs from the public, and wishes for a happy voyage and return from our assembled friends.

The following day was spent off Queenscliff in preparing for sea, and Friday, the 28th, saw us finally launched on the great voyage from which we hoped so much, and to which the previous moves formed only a prologue—at most, a first act.

What awaits us at and beyond the barrier of pack-ice which I have already forced so often in imaginary (and always successful) voyages? Shall we encounter the belt of ice 800 miles in width through which Sir James had to gain his second entry to the Great Bay, or will our steaming powers enable us to escape the dangers and incessant hardship so graphically reported by the great navigator ? Shall we meet the schools and shoals of Right whales described by him, and return with a full cargo and the just elation of the successful pioneer ?

Pacing the deck with the cheery second mate, with a good vessel under foot and a cheerful crew around us, the vivid remembrance of last year's success fills me with hope and elation at the nearness of the real battle.

The original Norwegian crew is now in a minority ; of the new hands, a number are Swedes, others are Danes, Poles, and Englishmen—a truly cosmopolitan and really fine set of men, the majority entering thoroughly into the spirit of the venture.

It was deemed too early in the season to attack the ice, and our plans therefore included a few weeks' sperm-whaling round Tasmania, and fur-sealing at Campbell and other islands before going South in earnest.

*October* 2.—After hailing the keeper of the lighthouse on Wilson's Promontory to know if

any whales had recently been seen, and obtaining
a negative reply, we continued our voyage to
Hobart Town, arriving this morning.

I here made the personal acquaintance of old
Mr. Hawthorn, with whom I had been in correspondence for several years. He returned my
visit in company with Mr. Bradley and Mr. Gill,
members of the Tasmanian Legislature, as well
as other colonial worthies, who all took a lively
interest in our vessel and enterprise.

*October* 3.—Left Hobart, and hovered round
South-west Cape for several days in search of
sperm whales ; they failed to keep the appointment.

Laid our course south for Royal Company
Islands. A strong westerly gale set us to the lee
of the group, storm and current preventing us
from regaining it. Bore away for Macquarie
Islands to essay our luck among fur-seals and
elephants.

*October* 13.—I to-day pass the meridian of life,
fifty years, and the fact becoming known, I am
pleased to receive cordial signs of goodwill from
officers and crew, the Captain treating the latter
in honour of the day.

As regards my relations with the Captain, it

will be understood that the past occurrences were not of a kind to be easily forgotten; but I was so impressed with the vital importance of at least an outward show of harmony and concord among the leaders of the expedition that I tried from first to last to suppress the remembrance of the past, and to co-operate with the Captain as loyally and cheerfully as it was in my power to do.

*October* 20.—We had failed to observe Royal Company Islands, although passing within sixteen miles of their reputed position, the wind being strong and the weather hazy at the time. Drifting weeds and a short, angry sea gave fair indications of neighbouring land. Many finners were seen. After a week of fine weather, we sight Macquarie to-day, and seek shelter from the strong north-wester under the lee of the island, where fairly calm water is met with. The aspect of the land is forbidding in the extreme, with barren cliffs descending perpendicularly into the sea; no foreshore or harbours visible.

The freshening gale puts an end to all thoughts of getting ashore. After standing by for three days, and sighting the grim island once more through the fog, we give up hopes of an early landing, and steer for Campbell.

Mr. Borchgrevinck's company has been of the greatest comfort to me during these weeks; we are thrown into close contact by the life on board our small ship, and tremendous schemes are laid for the future, after a triumphal return from the South.

*October* 25.—Sighted Campbell Island, and dropped our anchor in North Harbour during a strong westerly breeze. The next day is spent in coal-shifting and exploration of the land. Although a whole degree nearer to the Pole than Kerguelen, Campbell appears by comparison a very Eden : vegetation covers the island nearly to the top ; beautiful clinging shrubs and plants grow luxuriantly by themselves, or interweaving the groves of small trees which are twisted and crippled by the frequent gales. The volcanic character of the island gives it the same picturesque outlines which we have admired in Tristan, Crozet, and Kerguelen.

*October* 27.—Steamed round to Perseverance Harbour, falling in with a small schooner from New Zealand, with a crew of eight men and a cargo of 309 fur-seals. We receive a great shock on learning from Captain Josse that the season for fur-sealing opened on September 1, closing on November 1 ; we are thus left with four days

8

in which to complete our cargo. Could the New
Zealand Government have arranged this little
surprise specially for us after the visit by the
*Antarctic* to Campbell in July and August?

Late at night the second mate returned to the
vessel with three fur-seals. I was extremely
interested to meet in person the sea-bear or fur-
seal proper, as forming a link between the prehistoric, only half aquatic seals and the ordinary
present types, where the limbs have been so far
transformed as to render the usual gait of quad-
rupeds impossible. These poorer types of seals
no doubt consider the gait of the sea-bear extremely elegant and enviable, however comical
the effect is on the human mind.

The next day (Sunday) is spent in hunting and
exploration of the island by various parties, Mr.
Borchgrevinck returning with a satchel full of
plants and eggs. I spent the day in writing innumerable letters to my family and friends, posting
them by Captain Josse the next day. So far as
we know, this constitutes the last mail from the
*Antarctic* this year—and for all subsequent years,
should the ice hug us too tenderly.

Letters to my friends in Melbourne adjure
them to prepare the ground for the large com-

pany to be formed on our return with the vessel sinking with blubber and whalebone.

Mr. Borchgrevinck also works for the future by letters, the contents of which amuse me beyond measure, but which I do not feel justified in revealing. At this period—in fact, during the whole voyage—he treats me with grateful kindness.

We exchanged provisions with Captain Josse in return for skins, and obtained from this gentleman useful information about whaling round Solander, Kermadek, and Bounty Island, apparently a lucrative business in the right season.

Fur-sealing round Campbell and neighbouring islands was of considerable importance years ago, before indiscriminate slaughter had destroyed the rookeries ; the few animals left are hunted up from under stones, out of caverns, behind breakers, and wherever Nature affords a precarious shelter.

*October* 31.—Up anchor and out to sea, hugging the ugly precipitous shore as close as possible. Both mates are searching the coast from their boats ; but although the weather is remarkably fine, the breakers are falling and surging with great force, rendering the hunt very perilous.

Seven fur-seals and a few of the common varieties is the whole bag of the day, and the mate has in addition lost his boat, with its whale-line. Caught in the surf, the craft was flung broadside on against the rocks, and stove like an eggshell. The three occupants were saved with considerable trouble. One of our Danes was carried off his feet and out to sea three times before he could get a footing, hugging his rifle like a man the whole time. A Norwegian sailor also fell in the water from the slippery stones on trying to land, and was only recovered as he came to the surface for the third time—with little breath left in him.

This risky way of sealing is avoided by the New Zealand men, who lower themselves down the precipices from the plateau of the land, haul the animals out of their hiding-places with a crook staff, and despatch them with a club like a policeman's.

*November* 1.—The season being at an end to-day, we are heading away from Campbell and our unsuccessful hunt, laying our course for the doubt-ful Emerald Island. Weather magnificent.

*November* 5.—A great change in temperature of air and water was observed yesterday, indicating the neighbourhood of ice. The air registered only 38°, as against 42° F.; the water also 34°, previously 44°. The weather has hitherto been fair in the main, but to-day we have a northerly gale with barometric height of 28·7″. As an extract of the vessel's log is given at the end of the book, with a record of our observations day by day, I will in the following pages not tire my readers by enumerating temperatures, barometric heights, etc., but refer those interested in such matters once for all to the collated tables.

The albatross has now left us entirely. Schools of penguins have been passed on several occasions, proceeding in an easterly direction. We failed to sight Emerald Island—of doubtful existence.

At 7 a.m. we sight the first considerable iceberg in 56° 57′ S. lat., 162° E. long., estimated length five to seven miles, height 100 to 150 feet, perfectly flat top, colour bluish-white, changing into azure blue where the sea has hollowed out magnificent caves. The indescribable purity and transparency of colouring is particularly fascinating to those who behold the bergs for the first time.

More and more ice hove in sight as the day wore on. The smaller bergs appeared to be the sheddings of the larger ones, differing by their more irregular shapes from the nearly uniform type of the extended tabular masses. By their number they constitute a greater danger to navigation at night or in foggy weather than their parents, as the thermometer gives no warning. Even the streams of ice-blocks trailing for miles behind the large bergs, from which they are detached, are very dangerous, as the weight of many of the pieces is enough to stave in the bows of any vessel striking with fair speed, and not strengthened purposely to encounter shocks of this kind. Their lowness in the water makes it impossible to perceive them in dark nights or heavy fogs in time to avoid a collision.

Most of the bergs met with showed the regular stratification noticed by all other explorers of these latitudes.

The weather keeps fine, but night is still ruling from nine till three ; the moon is only a crescent, mist and rain are frequent, and a clear daybreak therefore the most acceptable weather for landsmen, until familiarity with the new surroundings breeds, not contempt, but a moderate degree of callousness.

We now realized the wisdom of having made a later start than advised by certain authorities. Had we listened to our great friend Baron von Mueller, and set off in September, the long nights would have largely increased our dangers, and the pack-ice would most likely not have been forced a day sooner, *vide* the experience in 1841-42 of Sir James Ross, and later on of ourselves.

*November* 6.—Low barometer ; wind increasing to a gale, with heavy squalls during night. At 4 p.m. we sighted a long, low island, flat on the top, but sloping up in one place to a greater height. It stretches away to a considerable extent in direction E. to W. and E. to S. We guess at Emerald Island, although we are a whole degree more southerly than the position indicated on the chart for that land. Its great length, estimated at about fifty miles, is also rather perplexing.

As we draw nearer, the Captain persuades himself that we have discovered new land. The crew is called together to greet it with a ' Hurrah !' and the christening, during which the name Svend Foyn Island is affixed to our discovery for all ages, is celebrated with a glass of brandy.

The disappointment was severe when it appeared that the immense tract was merely a floating iceland of—as far as I know—unprecedented dimensions. Its dirty-gray colour must excuse our mistake. We concluded that the colouring matter was of volcanic origin. It will be remembered that Captain Balleny observed smoke from the highest peak on the island group discovered by, and named after, him.    There is, then, a fair possibility that the floating island had its origin among the Balleny glaciers and ice-cliffs, or, at least, had stranded in their neighbourhood for a sufficient time to receive its layer of ashes or stone powder.

The discovery of new active volcanoes in regions where an iceberg of such dimensions could become, not only formed, but also detached and set afloat, may enable men of science to make a better guess in the future regarding the origin of what I believe is the largest floating mass of ice which has ever been met with.*

We estimated the height of the loftiest part of the berg at 600 feet at the time ; further experience in the ice led us to believe that this calculation was somewhat high, although a berg 960 feet in height has been met with in the Southern Ocean.    With 500 to 600 feet above water, and about 4,000 feet below, the immensity of the Svend Foyn Island can be roughly guessed at.

* The comparative shallowness of the sea at the bottom of South Victoria Bay renders it physically impossible that an iceberg of such thickness (height) could be set afloat in the vicinity of Mount Erebus.    The dirty layer must, therefore, have been acquired in a different neighbourhood.

On trying to approach the iceland closely we met with a choppy sea and eddies of such violence that we had to beat a hasty retreat. I do not believe that these eddies proved the whole mass to be really aground. Similar eddies and currents are experienced close to all extensive bergs.

The latitude of our discovery was 58° S. The first icebergs we met — as already stated — in 56° 57' S. Sir James observed his first ice in 63° 20' S. lat. in 1840, and in 58° 36' S. lat. during 1841.

We now have to navigate at night with the greatest caution. After clearing our immense friend and a few common bergs, we heave to, or proceed under shortened sail during the dark hours. Course easterly.

*November 7.*—Fair light wind. In the afternoon the engine is ordered ahead again, when, to our consternation, it begins racing away at a violent speed, and is then stopped up short. Our engineer comes up from below in great excitement. The propeller is either broken or loose on the shaft. What a frightful blow! Total disablement, except when the breeze will kindly assist us. Forcing the near pack-ice in our present condition would be, to my mind, sheer folly, although the Captain has rather a mind to try. On the other hand, our nearest harbour is Port Chalmers, New Zealand, 700 miles away. The delay in getting there, repairing our damage, and recovering our southing, will seriously prejudice our chance of penetrating the ice; in any case it will rob us of a month or more of the short season during which we have to force the pack, both coming and returning, and get our cargo, or look for it elsewhere, should our whaling beyond the ice prove a delusion.

It was decided to turn northwards again, and I had overcome my chagrin at the rebuff, when a new light thrown on the cause of accident upset my equilibrium for a long time. Imagine my sensation when the engineer told me that he had all along feared that the propeller, during the bumping at Campbell, had received some damage; that he had reported his fear to the Captain, and been asked not to trouble about the matter, as the damage might be trifling and things were sure to go all right.

I blamed him severely for not reporting to me as well in Melbourne, where a nominal sum would have sufficed to put all in order. Another fortnight would have seen us deep into the ice-pack—

possibly through it—where a loose propeller would have meant a fair possibility of wintering once, if not for ever, and at least ruin of our chance of commercial success. Even pioneers take some little stock of their lives ; I cannot, therefore, feel much repentance for my bitter feelings at the time.

*November* 8.—Our accident happened in 59° 20′ S. lat., 163° 50′ E. long. We are at present crowding on every stitch of canvas to the light breeze in our retreat from the near battlefield. The mist, lifting at times, unveiled to us once more the grand but awful Svend Foyn Island. Minor bergs in the neighbourhood appear to have recently detached themselves from the mass. Beautiful clear weather in the evening, during which Mr. Borchgrevinck is hard at work in the cabin, sketching the ice.

Our accident is too recent to allow a full enjoyment of the magnificent spectacle of a sunset among the icebergs ; the silence in the engine-room corresponds too well with our gloomy frame of mind, but it is imperative to put a brave face on it, and not depress the crew with our own feelings ; so hope on, hope ever.

*November* 9.—The day of my silver wedding. I feel justified in seeking refuge from the troubles of the present in the happy memories of the past—for this day only.

The Captain again talks about going South in our present condition. I do not trouble to argue the matter with him.

*November* 13.—On the 9th the wind freshened to half a gale, veering round to the south, and is now blowing a strong gale, with the barometer at one time down to 28″, the lowest reading since our departure.

In spite of the heavy sea, we run before the wind at a great speed. A few days more of the same will carry us to our destination. The vessel behaves in her former noble manner, lifting like a duck after every send into the trough.

*November* 15.—Sighted yesterday the Snares, later on the Traps, small groups of barren rocks, their names being a true index to their character. Stewart Island is seen to-day.

*November* 25.—The last week has been one of calms and contrary winds, with tedious tacking and small progress. It is more serious, however, that a sullen and ill-boding spirit is prevailing among the crew ; discipline is not perfect. I really do not believe that a single contented or happy being is found on board.

*November* 26.—I landed with the pilot - boat at the semaphore - station, telephoned to Port Chalmers for a tug, and instructed the Dry Dock officials to be ready for us next morning.

*November* 27.—The vessel is in dock, and the accident found to be due to the loosening of the key. We had secured the loose propeller at sea as best we could, and no damage whatever can be traced to the severe blows which it nevertheless gave our stern frame in the heaving and hoisting of the mountainous waves.

The work proceeded all night, and we could warp out of dock again by ten o'clock the next morning (Wednesday). Having telegraphed to Melbourne for money, I could pay for tugs, dock, fitting, etc., in all about £100, and we are ready for another start.

The reply from my agents in Melbourne authorizing the necessary credit had not been received at Dunedin at the closing time of the local bank, but the manager, with great kindness, instructed the cashier to remain at the offices, and on receipt of the telegram the money was handed to me, although the wording was far from clear.

In the night a Colonial and a Swedish sailor deserted us by swimming ashore. On Thursday six of the crew refused to proceed with the ship for divers reasons, and to avoid annoyance the Captain allowed them to go.  The Danish steward also had enough of it, and we now counted nine hands less than at our start from Melbourne. We got under way at 2 a.m. Friday, to avoid losing more hands.

At this point I must ask leave to make a confession.  During the voyage to New Zealand I had been pondering what the result would be on Commander Foyn's mind when the news should reach him of our fresh disaster, even more unpardonable than the shipwreck, and I came to the conclusion that he would immediately order us home in the first outburst of justifiable anger.  (The correctness of my conclusions was fully ascertained by me when I finally arrived home.) Under any ordinary circumstances my loyalty to him would have led me to telegraph him, and chance the consequences ; but as our damage was more annoying and exasperating than serious— although it might appear different when communicated by a short telegram only—I took upon myself to ask Reuter's agent in Port Chalmers to delay his message reporting our misfortune for a day or two, until we were beyond recall.

The damage to the vessel being so trifling, I was quite within my rights, as the manager abroad, to act in this way; still, I quite admit that I took a little more on myself than I perhaps ought to have done, in view of Mr. Foyn's great confidence in me, and must tender my apologies herewith to the representatives of the owners. To carry out the exploration of the Great Bay stood at the time before me as the paramount duty, and the accident had not altered the possibilities of our quest in any way.

I feel more happy at sea, with our bow pointing the right way again, but the Captain's vacillation and evident despondency is now becoming a real danger to the expedition. The intention was to call at Stewart Island to complete our crew; now he wants to go south as we are; another moment he would prefer to go straight home to Norway. I have to preach, argue, and implore him to keep such idle thoughts to himself, in order to shame him into a better frame of mind. What reception should we get in Norway? Should we not appear suspiciously like whipped dogs? Where is now the toughness and tremendous fortitude of Norwegians under difficulties? How can we preserve the respect and discipline of the crew if the leaders make an abject exhibition of themselves by wailing in public?

The result of my oratory was not perfect, but at any rate we called at Stewart Island, and obtained four additional hands. We are now twenty-six on board all told, and going due south. There is still much trouble with the crew, but I fully believe that serious work in the ice will again bring out all their better qualities.

*November* 29.—How little it takes to change the tone and feeling on board a vessel! The fair breeze has carried us along at a spanking rate; interest, goodwill, and good humour return. The new hands appear to be an acquisition, especially Mr. Joss, an old, experienced whaler, accustomed to harpooning and lancing, and, most important of all, very cheery.

*December* 2.—We have made famous progress before the steady favouring wind. Our latitude is to-day 56° S. In a few days we shall have recovered the southing gained at the time of our accident. Can the delay have been a blessing in a very rough disguise, and our coming progress through the ice be even furthered by the lateness of the season? The experience of Sir James Ross during his last voyage almost makes the idea probable, and at any rate the interest and courage of all must be kept up by every justifiable argument.

We now approach the field where Sir James fell in with the first Right whales, and the tension among the crew is quickly rising to the correct working pitch.

Borchgrevinck to-day completes his thirtieth year, and we celebrate the event with a heavy meal of rice fritters.

*December 3.*—Sighted the first iceberg at one o'clock this morning, S. lat. 58°, E. long. 166° 55′; to-day a number more are passed. Fog and strong breeze from W.S.W.

*December 4.*—Brilliant weather; a single great iceberg in sight. At noon our observation makes our position 61° 11′ S. lat., 171° E. long.; we have therefore passed the most southerly position attained during our first try. We have completed the double journey of 1,400 miles in twenty-seven days, counting in the time lost in harbour, and are now flying along before the pleasant breeze once more to attack the ice-belt, which is at length within a few days' sail.

# CHAPTER VIII.

### GRIPPED BY THE ICE.—BALLENY ISLANDS.— CHRISTMAS IN THE PACK.

*December* 6.—We advance rapidly southwards, with icebergs in all directions, although not in great numbers. The mist, as a rule, prevents us from seeing far, but when the sun at intervals can break his way through, the view around us is enchanting. Many of the surrounding bergs now present very fantastic forms, with deep caverns of the already described intensely blue and pure scheme of colour. The tabular icebergs are, however, still in the majority.

Yesterday several blue (finned) whales were sighted. This morning at 5.30 the mate brought us on deck with a run by reporting a Right whale off our counter, but the only animal now in sight is soon made out to be a hump-backed whale—a common variety in the Arctic

seas—and the disappointment is great. The
carpenter assures us that he also observed a
Right whale, and we are left in doubt for the
present.

*December* 9.—During the last days we have
sailed through large masses of scattered ice-floes
and streams of pack-ice, consisting of broken
floes with heavy layers of snow. Our experienced
sealers declare this ice to be the produce of last
winter's cold. The white petrel and gray Cape
pigeon announce the neighbourhood of the pack-
ice proper.

Our first seals were brought on board on
December 7—a common seal and a sea-leopard,
presumably of the variety captured south of Cape
Horn by the Scotch and German expeditions.
The skins appear to be of very good quality.

The ice floes did not exhibit the remarkable
heaped-up condition due to ' screwing ' which is so
well known in Arctic seas.

Yesterday the Captain reported that he had
seen a Right whale so clearly that no doubt could
exist as to its genuineness—a great encourage-
ment to us all.

The weather is to-day foggy, with falls of snow.
We are lying still ; and close but thin ice is seen

around as far as the eye can reach when occasional rifts in the mist give an opportunity.

My first days in the ice have been extremely interesting, but the continual bumping against the heavier pack, and the violent shocks to the vessel, are an experience to which a middle-aged lands-man does not become accustomed in a day. It is incredible that any structure can withstand this interminable series of collisions of a force under which the hull is trembling from stem to stern, and the masts bending, whilst you are flung bodily forward unless you are on guard. The ship forges ahead under sail and steam, the heavy column of smoke proving a magnificent contrast to the blinding whiteness of the floes as it is borne away and slowly dispersed by the wind.

The doubtful observation obtained yesterday made our position 65° 47′ S. lat., and about 171° 30′ E. long. ; adding the few miles of south-ing gained during the night, we are now under 66° S. lat.

*December* 10.—Completely surrounded by ice ; many bergs ; gale of S.W. raging ; the wind penetrates through my complete armour of pea jacket, three guernseys, and a heavy shirt, although the thermometer is merely down to 32°.

IN THE LEE OF A BERG AND PACK ICE.

Query : How many jackets, guernseys, and shirts will be required in an Antarctic winter gale, with the thermometer many degrees below zero ?

The floes are packed so closely that no swell can reach us, and you have a sensation of being in dock, with a howling storm pulling at your rigging in vain. The rest from the eternal bumping is very acceptable. Barometer 28·2″.

*December* 11.—The sun appeared at noon. Latitude by observation 66° 48′ S. Barometer still down to 28·4″, but the gale has abated, and the ice opened, showing patches of clear water ahead. We prepare to advance towards Balleny Islands, hoping to find both whales and seals.

*December* 12.—Magnificent weather, fresh and clear, crisp air giving no chance to bacilli and bacteria, be their names and forms as wonderful as the microscope and imagination of scientists can scare us with.

Saw a number of blue whales, and harpooned two from the vessel, the line breaking like a piece of twine on becoming taut. My belief in the black whales of Sir James Ross is getting a little shaken ; it is strange that we should not have fallen in with a single undoubted specimen (I make free to put the Captain's Right whale in

the same doubtful category as the mate's).   Could
Sir James have mistaken blue whales for black?

The sea is remarkably free from ice at present;
the scattered floes do not hinder our progress.
But for its great variations in temperature, the
cabin is very comfortable.   When the steward
fills the stove the thermometer quickly runs up
to 110° F.; after a few hours it is down to 70°,
when it is again sent up to 110°, and so on.

The panels of the doors are being covered by
Mr. Borchgrevinck with pictures of the surrounding scenes, to eternalize the memory of our
expedition.

Our position is by doubtful observation 65° 29′
S. lat. (?), 170° E. long.

A boat has been lowered several times to-day
to capture a single seal, much precious time being
lost by these manœuvres.

The bird-life around is a source of continual
entertainment.   The birds continue to be the
same as described by Sir James Ross—petrels of
several varieties, gulls, etc.   With the ice, water,
seals, whales, and bird-life there is never a second
in Antarctic (or Arctic) navigation during which
the surroundings do not lay claim to your attention and interest.   Time flies, in spite of the days

lengthening until they occupy the whole of the twenty-four hours.

On nearing and entering the pack, the birds peculiar to the closer floe-ice had made their appearance. The most fascinating among them must always be the white petrels, which are noticed hovering or gyrating round the vessel throughout the twenty-four hours apparently without retiring for rest or sleep ; their graceful flight and snowy plumage are always equally captivating to the eye. We noticed apparently two varieties, differing in size, unless the variation was merely due to the difference in sex.

The gray Cape pigeon is common. We also frequently noticed another variety of this bird, somewhat larger in size, and with brownish-coloured wings. I shot one of them from the deck. It is now in a Melbourne museum.

Besides the varieties of petrels, we also met with penguins in large numbers of the varieties already described during our stay at Kerguelen. The common penguin was by far the most frequent, the large king penguin being only seen on a few occasions.

*December* 13.—Weather continues fine, although cloudy. We steam S.W., fetching on board a stray seal from time to time. The Captain is already losing hope at the absence hitherto of seals and whales in any considerable numbers.

*December* 15.—Weather still superb ; steering for Balleny Islands, which we sight in the evening, despite our doubtful observations during the last few days. The heavy atmosphere prevents a fair view of the group, but at midnight the snow-clad peak (12,000 feet high) of the chief island is observed above the cloud-banks.

We hove-to during the night, hoping to get under the land in daytime and find seals ; but the ice, which is here of a much heavier character, had closed upon the vessel in the morning. If we are beset, a serious delay may follow, and we therefore seek clearer water in an easterly direction, hoping that the whales may compensate us for missing the elephants. A few seals are picked up as we go along. The surface of the floes is covered with a deep layer or layers of snow, which made the work in trudging after the seals extremely laborious.

*December* 17.—The close and heavy ice stopped our progress in the night of the 15th, since when the floes have kept us closely imprisoned. Yesterday evening the wind increased, with heavy squalls during the night, and a dangerous rolling of the ponderous blocks, which are gripping us and shaking the vessel with their angry blows. An attempt to press on towards the east is ineffectual, and we are now made fast with our strongest hawser to a great ice-floe, which acts to some extent as a buffer. The ice is stretching without a clearance beyond the horizon. During the darker hours the restless filing and pounding of the ice cannot but fill a landsman with anxiety, although our cheerful second mate declares that we are lying 'as comfortable as in an eiderdown bed.'

We are shifting coals to-day from tanks to bunkers, and find that the last fortnight has made a great inroad upon our supply.

I have to cheer up myself and everybody to the best of my powers ; but the scarcity of seals, and the lack of order and discipline at the guns when we have had a chance of harpooning whales, is very dispiriting.

*December* 19.—Weather moderately fair, with light breeze of W. and N.W. No open water anywhere. The ice appears to slacken, but our progress is painfully slow. Course S.E. No observation to be got. Our move towards Balleny was most likely a mistake. In 173° to 175° Sir James met considerably more open water — eighteen days later in the season, however.

Our remaining supply of coals is found to be eighty tons (approximately). To save enough for whaling beyond the ice-belt, and for emergencies, we must rely as much as possible on our sails in forcing the rest of the pack.

*December* 20.—The pack is as close as ever, and the floes and blocks of greater dimensions than at any time previously; weather fair, and inconsiderable swell. The wind freshening to a stiff breeze of N.W., we make a determined attempt to get free in the afternoon, every sail set, and the engine kept working to assist us. Got into much slacker and smaller ice towards night. Observation at noon gave 66° 15′ S. lat., 165° 5′ E. long.; trying our utmost to increase our easterly longitude.

Sighted in the evening one of the Balleny Islands once more, apparently Young's Island; same outline as the land observed a few days previously, distance sixteen to eighteen miles. At twelve o'clock at night, the midnight sun is just skimming the horizon, and it is perfectly easy to read in bed.

KILLING SEALS.

Nearly one-half of the seals captured proved of no value as regards their skins, which were lacerated in a peculiar manner, the scars frequently running parallel, up to twelve inches in length, and about an inch apart, chiefly on the sides and lower portions of the body. I shall return to this matter in a subsequent chapter, and will therefore here merely state that the scars were rarely, if ever, found on the sea-leopards we killed, as if the size of this animal rather awed the mysterious enemy of his smaller cousins, but they were particularly frequent on the whitish-yellow or light gray seal which goes under the name of the white Antarctic seal, though it is never found of such whiteness that it cannot readily be distinguished on the ice-floes.

The sealing in Antarctic waters offers no more excitement to the sportsman than at Kerguelen ; the seals on approach are either found in a state of peaceful slumber, or look on with mild curiosity as the rifle is levelled. The killing is therefore particularly repugnant even to a hardened sealer ; the complete trustfulness of the Antarctic seal on the ice or land indicates that no enemy, ' huge ' or small, ever pursues it above water.

We secured on our voyage through the ice

seals of all the varieties described by Sir James Ross as met with in the same regions, including a single specimen of the interesting earless species.

*December* 21.—We are steaming N.E. into lighter and more scattered ice, picking up a few stray seals in passing, at great loss of time and coals —to me a most irritating performance in our serious position.   Latitude 66° 13′ S.

*December* 22.—The weather keeps wonderfully calm and fine ; whatever swell there may be outside, the most languid rolling only penetrates to us.   Course N.E. ; a light breeze of N.W.

The scenery at eleven last night, as the dipping sun lighted up the cone of Balleny Island, was extremely beautiful—more like a dream than reality. I took a photograph of the view.   Distance of land about twenty-five miles.

The manœuvring of the vessel is criticised by our experienced men in more forcible than elegant language.

We should, in my opinion, push on day and night, regardless of coal-consumption, whenever the ice slackens, instead of stopping the engine during long intervals at night.

We make good progress to-day from one open space to another through quantities of loose ice.

Harpooned a blue whale this afternoon, which ran out two lengths of lines, and promptly broke the 'painter' as it grew taut; the omission this time consisted in not firing the bomb-gun for some reason or other. Killing the blue whale on the spot is our only chance; firing the two guns simultaneously appears a feat beyond our capacity, and the outlook in respect of blue-whaling is therefore very black indeed.

Position at noon by observation, 66° 3' S. lat., 167° 37' E. long. The ice appears endless.

*December* 23.—Weather continues fine; light to fresh breeze from W. or W.S.W. Advancing under steam and sail through large masses of ice and numbers of bergs, many of great size. The sun during its setting towards the horizon, under which it now never sinks, gave us last night another view of wonderful beauty; when the engine is stopped at such times, the endless white, the purity of the colouring, and the all-pervading silence, give you a feeling of gliding through a fairyland, until a bump, or the hoarse cry of a sea-bird, awakens you to a very stern reality.

In spite of its being Sunday, we harpooned a small whale, called in the Arctic language a Mencke whale, after a German who accompanied

Mr. Foyn on some of his voyages.   Under a
commotion and uproar worthy of a Right whale,
the animal is killed and brought alongside; its
value is very small, except for the practice it
gives our men, and the excellent steaks which it
adds to our larder.   The scenes of frying and
feasting in the evening must have resembled in
many respects the epilogue to a successful hunting
expedition by cannibals whose stock of missionary
has been long exhausted; the meat is tied up in
chunks under the boats, and everyone is welcome
to carry away and prepare for eating as much as
he likes whenever he feels empty.

Our sealing parody has now resulted in a total
catch of sixty-five animals, and unless we can fall
in with proper herds, our only chance is evidently
whaling.   The idea that such herds or rookeries
might be found round Balleny Islands is our excuse
for getting so far west, a proceeding which has
cost us dear.

*December* 25.—Christmas Day.   Position by
observation, 66° 32' S. lat., 170° 25' E. long.   We
yesterday forged ahead under sail and steam as
hard as we could drive the vessel.   Course S.
and S.E.   Ice fairly slack.   The Christmas Eve
is celebrated with 'cream porridge' (made with

butter) in the orthodox manner, and Mencke whale in divers forms. The tone among the crew is not bad, considering our tribulations and disappointments.

*December* 26.—Fast in the ice, which extends apparently without limit. Position 66° 55′ S. Weather cold, with a strong breeze to half a gale of wind. No rolling perceptible in the ice.

Mr. Borchgrevinck is busy preparing bird-skins and stuffing others. The white petrels are everywhere, lending a particular charm to the near landscape, harmonizing as they do with the colouring, and graceful in every motion.

*December* 27.—Our position to-day is 66° 37′ S. lat., 171° 15′ E. long. The painful struggle with the ice can be measured by comparing the successive observations. The drifting of the ice when we are closed in, and our efforts to get eastwards away from the fatal neighbourhood of Balleny, result in our losing one day whatever increase of southing we have gained the day before. Our only consolation is that the whole mass of ice is drifting northwards at a fair speed, so that by merely maintaining our position we approach day by day to the southern edge of the pack.

The Captain has reefed a steel hawser instead

of whale-line, and thinks that he will now be able to hold the blue whale. I have seen enough blue-whaling not to think much of the dodge. As a matter of fact, it did not get a practical trial.

The weather is magnificent, with warm sunshine and light breeze from S.E.; but we now have to consider at times the possibility of being unable to get through the pack, a melancholy idea which I dismiss whenever possible. Imagine that Sir James in 1839-40 broke through the belt in five days with two sailing-vessels. We have now been eighteen days in the pack, and have practically not advanced an inch during the last fortnight.

*December* 28.—The pressure of the ice relents a trifle. We progress in a south-easterly direction. No observation. Estimate our longitude at 173° E., lat. at 66° 30′ S.

Harpooned a small Mencke whale, which ran out a long coil of rope, and finally escaped, the propeller having cut the line. We captured five seals during the day. Clouds of white petrels and Cape pigeons around us. The shocks on colliding with the ice are at times appalling, but no one cares about anything at present but to get away from the choking grip of the ice.

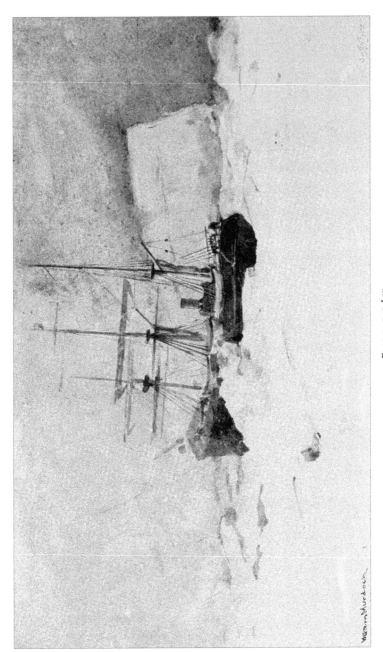

FAST IN THE ICE.

A most distressing accident happened in the afternoon to our excellent first engineer. In trying to get the shaft 'on the centre,' which is done by turning it round with a heavy crowbar, the engine suddenly made a turn ahead instead of astern, as contemplated. The bar struck our friend, tore off the tip of his left index-finger, and broke his right leg just above the instep.

The mate, assisted by a few others, performed a very creditable setting of the leg, during which our brave fellow uttered no complaint beyond remarking that 'he had got a poor birthday present.' He chanced to complete his twenty-eighth year on the very day of the accident. The finger presented a very miserable sight, but he had no sympathy whatever to spare for this if he could only have escaped fracturing his leg.

We did all in our power to make him comfortable, but it will be understood how unsuitable a whaler, pounding against the ice by night and day, must be as a hospital in this kind of ailment. Pacing freely on the deck, with the light flooding us, and breathing the crisp air, it was very melancholy to consider the position of the poor man confined with his broken leg for weeks to his stuffy cabin, where lamplight was the only illumination, day or night.

The accident would have depressed us all at any time, but caused additional gloom during this time of anxiety for the future.

*December* 29.—We are now well to the east, but find the ice closing up so firmly as to stop all progress. Floes rather large. Weather continues equally brilliant, with a high barometer. Position by observation 66° 56' S. lat., 172° 46' E. long.

*December* 30.—We are held firmly in the pack ; no open water to be seen. The ice may slacken for a short time, and narrow strips of water appear between some of the floes, but we can make no impression on the barrier. The outlook at the end of the year is gloomy in the extreme, the enforced idleness increasing the depression. Our only consolation is that the poor engineer gets a little rest for his leg, thanks to which his symptoms of fever diminish, and he is getting on better than we dared to hope under the unfavourable circumstances.

*December* 31.—The last day of the good old year, so rich in both success and adversity.

Our position to-day—66° 47' S. lat., and

174° 13′ E. long.—reveals the fact that we are again drifting northwards.

The appearance of the ice is extremely dispiriting. It is wedged close together as far as we can see, gripping our good vessel firmly between heaped-up floes, with hardly a square foot of water anywhere between them. The engine is stopped, and the silence and general sense of desolation pervading the surroundings oppress your heart as you contemplate the present and the future.

The spirits of everyone are now at a low ebb. The crew are naturally much depressed at our apparent failure, and the company in the cabin are melancholy in the extreme.

And so departs the old year, with a general feeling of gloom in cabin, forecastle, and engine-room, and an outlook for the expedition which justifies much anxiety, however much I struggle to buoy up the courage and spirits of myself and the officers and crew.

## CHAPTER IX.

*January* 1, 1895.—We had gone to bed in the
cabin last night, when the chiming of the ship's
bell and the discharge of a gun signalled the
departure of last year, and brought us on deck.
The flag was run up under the gaff, and the birth
of the New Year greeted with further chiming
and a gun-salute. With the midnight sun flooding us with her rich yellow and red, the appearance of the scene was quite gay and festive. We
exchange wishes for a happy New Year, and
retire once more to our narrow cribs, hoping that
our wishes may come true, and the glorious birth
of the New Year be a good omen.

The day bids fair to fulfil the promise of the
night; the ice is considerably slacker over a wide
range. We advance through heavy streams of ice,
from pond to pond; direction of our course S.E.

Observation at noon 66° 50′ S. lat., 174° 16′ E. long. ; we have thus nearly recovered our most southerly position.

*January* 2.—We drifted with the ice and wind during the greater part of the night in an easterly direction. Half a gale with severe squalls, but no trace of rolling, which proves that we are still far from the edge of the pack. We advance painfully to-day through heavy and closer ice, using the propeller at intervals.

In spite of yesterday's progress, our position at noon is merely 67° 5′. The service on New Year's Day was much appreciated, although the singing is very poor when the carpenter—our leader—does not happen to know the melodies. I have kept up the service regularly every Sunday, and feel sure this has brought us all nearer together, forming at least one bond of union between the very heterogeneous elements on board our vessel.

To-night the pack is again closing up ; westerly gale blowing.

The Mencke whale is still furnishing enormous supplies of steaks of a quality fit to put before a king. Penguins in large numbers continue to be seen, and a fine specimen is to-day killed and prepared for the Captain's collection.

*January* 3.—The westerly gale has continued throughout the night, as well as to-day. To our pleasant surprise, the pack has now separated in various directions, permitting us to sail and steam from 9 a.m. to 6 p.m. from one clear space to another. Observation : 175° 45′ E. long., estimated lat. 67° 20′ S.

Our collisions with the heavier blocks are extremely violent as we press on with a speed of four to five knots. No better proof could be had of the strength of our vessel than the callous manner in which she negotiates every difficulty. It is extremely interesting to watch the floes rearing on end, and being brushed aside as we break our way forward.

As far as we can judge, the ice has—at least during the last days—opened during the forenoons and closed again towards evening ; currents and tides will no doubt account for this phenomenon.

Our beautiful weather of December has now left us, and the strong wind has kept blowing without abating since January 2. We hope that the ice will in consequence be set in motion, and a way south even now be opened for us. The vanishing stock of coals is our most pressing anxiety; unless we are speedily released, we shall have no fuel left for whaling, and the return voyage through the relentless pack. The latter eventuality we contemplate rather calmly, as one of the necessary risks of an Antarctic voyage; but whaling without steam will be a poor affair.

*January* 4.—Fast in the pack; as no advance is possible, the day is used for cleaning the boiler. Half a gale from W.; cloudy. Our engineer is getting on well; his fortitude is beyond praise.

*January* 5.—Wind changed to S. and S.E.; fresh breeze. The ice appears to have scattered, forming a number of open ponds visible from the crow's-nest, chiefly towards the east. In a southerly direction the pack seems quite as firm as before. The weather becomes fine with a clear sky. Observation: 67° 23′ S. lat., 176° 31′ E. long. The boiler-cleaning is over, and we prepare to work forwards; course easterly.

The Captain is inclined to give up the struggle and turn back, in order to retrieve our failures by a hunt for seals in more westerly longitudes. I cannot advise this course; our instructions are explicit, viz., to explore the Great Bay. If we return now, the whole struggle must be gone through once more during next season.

As our prospects are now brighter, some of my readers may possibly find time to bestow a little sympathy on the writer in his capacity of a *raconteur* lost among the Philistines; it is no insult to my good shipmates to confess that I never met a less humorous set of men in my life. Heaven knows that I should have borne this cross in humble meekness had more vital matters been to my satisfaction. Still, on a long and anxious voyage the relaxation in telling or listening to a good story is an important factor in keeping your own and other people's minds from barren brooding; I therefore take some credit to myself for having at rare intervals even conquered the whole of our glum company in the cabin, and set them laughing heartily. At other times the atmosphere was beyond clearing; as you reel off a good story, grim or contemptuous silence chills you from the highest quarter (and when the Captain is silent, let no mate laugh), you get flustered, and miss your good points, or you laugh idiotically at them yourself, the thread of the story is lost, or gets knotted as the silence becomes audible, and you end by leaving the company to their own melancholia, swearing that you will never cast pearls before Norwegian sailors again.

You soon, however, forgive your otherwise superior neighbour his natal defect, and start once more ; but never shall I forgive them the shipwreck of the gem of all my stories, the true narrative of the Norwegian merchant who wished to pleasantly surprise his monkey-loving son on his birthday, and telegraphed to his London agent to ship him 1 or 2 monkeys by the next steamer. The story of how the telegram was read as 'Ship 102 monkeys next steamer'; of how the poor agent scoured all London and could only ship sixty-seven, writing soothingly by the same post that balance would go forward by next steamer ; the story of the unexpected arrival of the sixty-seven at the small town at 4 a.m., their descent on all the gardens in the neighbourhood, the frightful time spent by the good merchant before all the monkeys could be collected, and all the despoiled women appeased, etc., etc.—this story has never been told by me without bringing down the house, and its shipwreck in the cabin of the *Antarctic* constitutes, to my mind, a crime beyond forgiveness. Every brother *raconteur* will understand my bitter feel-

ings and appreciate the possibilities of this particular story : if your listener really must catch
his train, you can crowd the chief incidents into
the space of two minutes, firing the last volley as
he takes his ticket (to the wrong station).    If
your victim is at your mercy, say in an express
train stopping nowhere for hours, or on board a
vessel in the Arctic or Antarctic seas, the variations and expansions are without any other limit
than your victim's patience, nay, even beyond the
latter.

*January* 6.—Twelve minutes after midnight ;
weather magnificent, the sun ascending slowly
and grandly from its lowest point.   The peace
and stillness of the ice landscape is wonderfully
soothing ; the blowing of whales in different
directions, or the cry of the ever-circling white
petrels, form the only interruptions.   The birds
referred to apparently do not take either sleep or
rest throughout the Antarctic day and night.

But what is better than sun, petrels, and useless whales, is that we have been sailing for hours
through large ponds widening between the floes.
From the masthead, the way south appears opening to the horizon ; the ice-fences separating the
pieces of open water are scattered with ease before

our heavy ship. The wind is light, from S.W., making our progress slow; but we dare not make further inroads on our coal-supply.

'Pond' is a very suitable denomination for these spaces of open water, through which the vessel glides smoothly, undisturbed by wave or swell. Sir James escaped from the pack in latitude 68° 30′ S.—that is, only fifteen to sixteen miles south of our present estimated position. Is our time of trial over, and the extending ponds a true indication of open water? The morning will show.

*January* 6.—Weather continues fine, with sunshine; fresh westerly breeze, with much open water between long streams of pack. Several icebergs are met with. A new variety of ice-floes is now prevalent, large in area, and of considerable thickness, the height above the water-line being about twenty to thirty feet. We assume that this new formation is true 'land-ice'; its total thickness, 200 to 300 feet, indicates that many winters must have passed before it broke its connection with the shore and drifted out to sea.

About 8 p.m. the ice began closing up, hindering our progress; the weather grew misty, and we made fast to a heavy floe, awaiting better conditions. Caught five seals and a few penguins

during the day.   The latter give the men a good
run before they are captured; 'rowing' themselves along on the floes by aid of their flappers
to avoid the pursuer, they look extremely comical,
but attain a very good speed.

*January* 7.—Spaces of clear water are seen
from the crow's-nest towards the east; we use
our engine in trying to reach them.   Observation
yesterday, 67° 43′ S. lat.; to-day, 68° 6′ S. lat.,
177° 20′ E. long.   Sir James Ross, in 1841,
escaped from the pack in 68° 45′ S. lat. on
January 9, meeting the pack proper under 66° 55′
as against our 65°.

The outlook is once more becoming very
serious.   We advance to-night through narrow
channels with large floes around; no wind, steaming continually.   The floes are now thin, and extremely large in area, proving that the water has
not been in appreciable motion for a considerable
time, which again points to a large expanse of ice
in all directions; otherwise, the swell would have
reached the thin ice, and broken it up small.
This conclusion is very dispiriting, but for the
experience already gained of the great changes in
the ice conditions which take place during a surprisingly short time.

Chasing King Penguins.

*January* 8.—A day of boisterous weather ; gale from the east, with snow, during which we are glad to closely hug the large floe to which we are made fast. We had advanced quickly during the night, until the enormous floes began to close up about 4 a.m. We hoped that the gale would assist us, and open the floes ; but the total absence of motion is not hopeful, proving that the pack edge is still far away. A king penguin was caught to-day.

*January* 10.—The gale from S. and S.W. is still blowing. The pack appears firm, with a few narrow channels ; we are lying very snugly in a pond of fair extent. Position by observation yesterday, 68° 21′ S. lat., 176° 15′ E. long. ; to-day, 68° 7′ S. lat., proving serious loss by drifting.

The gale appears to have had an effect on the pack, which opens during the day, chiefly towards the north, but also towards south and south-west.

Our position has to-day been under anxious discussion, as the ice has now so frequently relaxed its grip, and tightened it again before any appreciable advance has been made.

Shall we keep on waiting for better conditions, or shall we turn back and try to retrieve our fortune by sealing to the west of Balleny ?

The Captain's mind is in a continual state of vacillation, and I agree with him that either horn of our dilemma looks very uninviting as a prospective seat.    He desires me, as the representative of Mr. Foyn, and part owner in the vessel, to decide for him.    Under other circumstances, with a different and more clearly defined authority, I should have felt called upon to do this.    Under present conditions, I dare not interfere with his decision and responsibility as Captain of the vessel, and I can only advise, as I have done in the past, supporting my counsel with the best arguments at my command—in the present case by the following :

Mr. Foyn has sent us a distance of 14,000 miles, with explicit instructions to examine and ascertain whether Right whales exist in paying numbers in the Great Bay as stated by Sir James Ross.

It appears, therefore, to me to be in the highest degree incumbent upon us to use every reasonable effort, and to exhaust every resource compatible with the safety of the vessel and crew, before giving up the struggle.

I opine that we can await the end of the current month without risk to the expedition, and I advise

therefore that we shall continue our battle with
the pack until February 1.

If we succeed in penetrating the ice barrier, the
instructions of our employer have been carried
out, even if no Right whales are found ; if the
whales are met with, but the advanced season
compels an immediate retreat, we can easily
break through the pack another year with a more
powerful vessel and better equipment.

If we turn back now, the present uncertainty
regarding the Great Bay as a profitable whaling-
ground remains unsolved ; the whole cost of the
expedition, and our weary struggle, will have been
utterly wasted ; we shall risk the grave displeasure
of Mr. Foyn, whose hatred of pusillanimity is so
well known ; and if we also fail to obtain a cargo
of seals (which the lateness of the season makes
very probable), the owner will have double cause
for irritation, and will undoubtedly be deterred
from further exertions.

With more certainty of finding seals to the
west of Balleny, I might advise differently ; but
where is our guarantee of falling in with them in
paying numbers ?

The statement by Lieutenant Wilkes, that he
met with 'many' sea-elephants in a certain lati-

tude and longitude, is all we have on which to rest our hopes.

One more argument : To secure a full cargo of whales, if the animals are found in the numbers described by Sir James Ross, will not occupy more than a couple of weeks. With our few hands, we cannot obtain a paying cargo of seals in less than four to five weeks, a period which the lateness of the season does not allow us to spend in hunting.

I do not, however, feel called upon to decide as to the actual route, a responsibility naturally pertaining to the nautical leader.

*January* 11.—Weather unsettled ; wind blowing successively from all points of the compass, and varying from half a gale to moderate breeze and calm. Occasional showers of snow.

Moored to a large floe, we kept drifting all day before wind and current. Captured altogether thirteen seals, of which six were found in one spot —the greatest number hitherto found in one herd.

*January* 12.—No seals are visible to-day. Blue whales are daily to be seen in all directions, but not a single black whale. Strained relations between Captain and crew. Our observation

SEALERS AT WORK IN THE MIST.

gave us 68° 7′ S. lat.—a great surprise, as we had anticipated a considerable loss of southing. A southerly current must therefore, in this longitude, have been strong enough to compensate our loss by drifting before the S.E. wind.

We made fast for the night to a large floe, after another blue whale hunt. We got within beautiful range, but the cannon was fired before the animal had actually reached the surface. The shell did not, therefore, explode ; and thus another whaling comedy terminated. When will our appliances be in order and worked in a disciplined manner ?

*January* 13.—Another whale-hunt. A large animal is rising within striking distance, but now the anchors on the foredeck prevent the harpoon-gun from being discharged. The bomb-gun is fired by itself. Result nil, as regards advantage either to ourselves or the poor whale.

Unless gun-drill is seriously undertaken even at this, the eleventh hour, I can see no chance of success, even if we penetrate the ice and find schools upon schools of Right whales.

Of blue whales, numbers are seen day and night. Twenty are frequently counted within a short time.

With a steamer as described in Chapter II.,

and proper transport vessels, it would be possible to quickly obtain full cargoes by hunting in the ponds.

The red 'shrimps' which constitute the whale's daily bread are seen here in the same countless myriads as in the Arctic seas.

When a floe is broken, they scatter for shelter in millions, reminding one of the animation in a disturbed ant - heap. They appear in a great measure to sustain all higher animal life in these regions, as the stomachs of the seals and penguins examined contain large quantities of them.

Observations for longitude to-day give our position as 176° 4″ E. Both yesterday and to-day a fair amount of rolling in the ice has been observed. Whether from N.W. or S.E. is a matter of divided opinion. In the latter case there is a possibility that we really are at last approaching the edge of the pack, the more so as the peculiar cloud or dark mist described in polar language as 'water sky' is observed towards the south.

5.20 *p.m.*—'Open water ahead!' The cry sends a peculiar thrill through us all. Can it really be possible? Our long struggle and frequent disappointments make us slow to believe. Will not the evening again find the floes closing up? But no : the ponds increase in size, and, after awhile, the water towards the south as far as we can see is perfectly clear, except for inconsiderable streams of ice. The entire horizon in the same direction now shows the characteristic ' water sky.'

The engine is stopped, and the sails are drawing well before a westerly breeze. The weather continues fine. There can be little doubt that our struggle with the ice-demon is now at an end, and the victory ours, not a minute too early, as it transpires that the Captain had finally made up his mind this morning to order a retreat unless the day brought us open water or certain promise of such. However great our humiliation at such a retreat would have been, I will allow that no one in the morning had the slightest idea of the nearness of our delivery.

The effect of our success on the crew and officers was equally magical. The spirit which I had admired on leaving Melbourne is now again awake, and the many unpleasant incidents in the ice are sunk or forgotten in the keen interest with which we look forward to our adventures in. the wonderful regions towards which the gate is at last opened.

Our position at noon is 68° 12' S. lat., 176° 59' E. long.   We entered the main pack on December 8, in 65° 45' S. lat., 171° 36' E. long.   Not counting the drift of the ice, the width of the barrier penetrated is therefore about 150 miles; reckoning on a drift northwards of ten miles per day, an addition of 360 miles will have to be made : total width, therefore, about 500 miles.   If the looser floes and blocks encountered since December 4 are reckoned in, the total width of drift and pack-ice penetrated is 700 miles.   Sir James Ross was battling for fifty-six days in breaking through the pack on his second voyage; but when it is considered that his crew and officers were specially picked men, whose living did not in any way depend on the success or failure of their undertaking, I cannot but admire the patience of our men, who until yesterday had good reason to assume that the thirty-six long days in the ice would have been all spent in vain, and that every reasonable chance of retrieving our misfortune in other directions had also been destroyed by the enormous delay and the lateness of the season.

*January* 14.—Observations at noon 69° 16' S. lat., 177° 30' E. long.   During the day we have fallen in with numerous streams of ice, and had to

steer an easterly course from one pond to another.
Loose floes and streams are seen in all directions,
but none of serious dimensions or firmness.
Brilliant weather, with breeze from the west.
Only a few whales are observed, from which we
conclude that they prefer the ice, with its millions
of red ' shrimps' and molluscs.

We lay our course for Possession Island, in the
hope of meeting there the ' numerous whales' of
' unusual size' described by Sir James Ross. The
engineer continues to do well, but thinks it very
hard to have to listen to the more hopeful stories
of our progress without power to stir from his dark
hole to see the open water.

*January* 15.—After considerable forcing of ice
during the night, we emerge at last into perfectly
clear water at 4 a.m. What a strange sensation,
to survey the enormous expanse of water ahead
of us without eyeing a single piece of ice beyond
a small boat-shaped floe on which four penguins
sail northwards as passengers!

Our position when leaving the last floe behind
us is reckoned to be 69° 55′ S. lat., 177° 50′; but
our observation at noon gives us 70° 18′ S. lat.,
and the chronometer at 4 p.m. 175° 19′ E. long.
We have advanced the whole forenoon over a

surface unrippled by the faintest breeze, an almost imperceptible swell alone reminding us of the recent gale. The weather is magnificent, with warm sunshine. In the afternoon we are assisted by a gentle breeze, increasing until towards evening we can dispense with the assistance of the engine. A few blue whales have accompanied us, on two of which we have had evil designs ; but the propeller appears to frighten them, and we cannot get within range. Their voyaging southwards is looked upon as hopeful, and confirming the description by Sir James Ross of Cape Adare as a kind of trysting-place for whales in summer-time.

Before closing the chapter, I once more bring into comparison the experience of Sir James Ross in 1839-41, and of ourselves in 1894-95, regarding the conditions of the ice ; no better illustration can be given of the extreme variations with which the Antarctic navigator must reckon.

Sir James Ross, in 1841, entered the main pack January 5 in 66° 50′ S. lat., 174° 34′ E. long., clearing the last barrier on the 9th in 68° 45′, 176° 15′ E. long.—five days ; total width of pack about 170 miles.

In his next voyage, he began his attack on the

ice-belt on December 18, 1841, in 60° 50′ S. lat., 147° 23′ W. long., emerging into clear water on February 1, 1841, in 67° 18′ S. lat., 158° 12′ W. long.—fifty-six days ; width of pack upwards of 800 miles.

We struck the main pack on December 8, 1894, in 65° 45′ S. lat., 171° 36″ E. long., gaining clear water on January 13, 1895, in 68° 12′ S. lat., 176° 59′ E. long.—thirty-six days ; width of ice-belt about 500 miles.

At the risk of appearing ungrateful, I must state as my opinion that the very fineness of the season in 1894 was our worst enemy ; the terrible weather experienced by Sir James Ross increased the dangers and anxieties of his work in the ice, but also increased his opportunities of advance through the consequent disturbances of the pack. That we met with an ice-belt of rare width and closeness also appears from the fact that Sir James hardly ever felt any benefit from the surrounding ice during the gales, but nearly lost his vessels on account of the tremendous rolling of the ponderous blocks, whilst our ship rode off gale after gale in perfect comfort owing to the width and closeness of the barrier.

## CHAPTER X.

*SOUTH VICTORIA LAND.—POSSESSION ISLANDS.—
FIRST LANDING ON THE ANTARCTIC CONTINENT.*

*January* 17.—Early this morning the first sight
of the mysterious Antarctica is obtained : Mount
Sabine, with its summit 10,000 feet in height,
overtopping the bold mountain ranges which
gradually develop themselves before our eyes as
we approach the land, with its numberless peaks
and pinnacles, the whole landscape buried under a
snow-shroud of incomparable whiteness, without a
break except in a few exposed places along the
coast where the wind has been able to bare the
dark rock at intervals.

We lay our course towards the most prominent
of these partially-bared patches of land—Cape
Adare, the eastern extremity of the Continent ;
with its dark sides and snow-streaked top, about
4,000 feet high, it forms an excellent landmark.

We arrived under the cape about noon, but the easterly gale compelled us to haul off and await an improvement in the weather before attempting to land. Along the whole of the shore is a belt of ice-floes, which we hope to find penetrable.

Between Cape Adare and the land towards N.W., a small bend is observed—Robertson's Bay—which appears to form a good harbour, as it is free from ice; but a heavy barrier of heaped-up floes, with stranded bergs, are barricading the inlet, so we dare not attempt to run the blockade for fear of being caught and beset. A landing must therefore be delayed.

A dozen large bergs of considerable height, 100 to 200 feet, are lying stranded off Cape Adare; one of them greatly resembles a fortress with regular port-holes, and must have been stranded a considerable number of years for the action of the sea to have effected such a change from the usual solid square and regular type of Antarctic bergs.

*January* 18.—We steamed towards the shore through a channel in the pack with the intention of trying to land with one of the boats. During our approach, it, however, became evident that the tide was forcing the pack southwards at a great speed, and that all passages would rapidly be closed; a sealing-party was signalled back, and reached us through the last few feet of open water. As we steamed at full speed out of the channel with the boat towing astern, the floes closed up with considerable force. Had a party been landed, they would have been exposed to much hardship before they could have been recovered.

We ran before the strong breeze towards the west, intending to look for whales off Cape North, but the wind coming westerly in the evening, the course was laid for Possession Islands. The night was enchanting, with the glorious midnight sun illuminating the lofty mountain-ranges, which glittered and sparkled with a whiteness beside which the ice-floes—our previous standard of perfect white—appeared dull.

Several of our boats pursued in vain three pie-bald whales of a species unknown to us, their chief characteristic being a dorsal fin of disproportionate length. This species was also observed and commented upon by Sir James Ross.

*January* 19.—The westerly breeze slackening during the night, we repassed Cape Adare under sail and steam, and sighted presently our goal— Possession Islands, 71° 56′ S. lat. The wind again freshened to half a gale, and drove us ahead at a great speed. A fair number of ice ribbons extended in various directions; many large bergs were to be seen all around, several being stranded along the shore.

From the edge of the water, the land rises to enormous altitudes, with a covering of external snow; the dark patches of rock jutting out are either seen very sparsely inland, where the wind has been able to expose them, or more generally along the shore, where large masses of hard snow or ice could be clearly noticed to have broken away, baring the underlying rock. My photographs of the coast scenery unfortunately turned out particularly poor; otherwise, the next expedition would, by comparing the pictures of the shore, have definitely settled whether the whole towering uplands may not be looked upon as one continuous glacier overflowing at numerous points into the sea.

Above a comparatively insignificant altitude, the snow covering is continuous without the slightest break.

I take it that the icebergs of more fantastic and irregular forms are sheddings from this kind of glaciers, whilst the more numerous bergs, table-topped, with regular forms and perpendicular sides, are, I assume, born of the enormous barriers discovered in various latitudes along the Antarctic shores, where the upland is rising much more gently than is the case in the regions so far examined by us. Some of the irregular bergs must, I suppose, also be simply tabular bergs which have stranded and after years of corrosion under water have again got afloat and toppled over.

We were close under Possession Islands at 8 p.m., when a party consisting of the Captain, second mate, carpenter, Borchgrevinck, and others, rowed ashore to pay a visit to the natives— thousands of penguins, which could be seen from the deck to occupy nearly the whole extent of one of the islands. They found the colony as it no doubt appeared in 1840 to Sir James Ross and his party, the foundation consisting of an extensive heap of guano mixed with pebbles and bones of penguins, carried off by a natural or violent death, chiefly the latter, as the numerous predatory skua gulls look upon the colony as a private and inexhaustible larder, from which they draw their supplies in the form of young penguins with the utmost insolence and contempt for parental feelings. The myriads of colonists are drilled to the same degree of perfection which excited our wonder in other penguins' rookeries. In spite of their bewildering numbers, all their functions of life ashore are carried out with perfect absence of confusion; the only scenes of disorder are caused by an occasional attack from skua gulls, when the old ones are 'played' by some of the robbers, whilst others quietly haul away and despatch the screaming youngsters with a few savage pecks from their powerful bills.

The landing-party returned at midnight highly delighted with their trip, and bringing with them a collection of penguins and stones, as well as guano. The coffee and food kept in readiness was much appreciated after their exertions, and a general gossiping-party preceded our late retirement to bed. Samples of lichen found by Mr. Borchgrevinck in sheltered nooks on the island constituted the most interesting result of the landing, as it upset the previous theory of botanists, that the rigour of Antarctic winter was fatal to all vegetable life.

But where are the numbers of Right whales met with by Sir James in this particular spot? I have spent most of the time in an anxious look-out, and have not been rewarded by noticing the blowing of a single black whale. It is difficult, not to say impossible, to hope against hope any longer; Sir James may have mistaken blue whales for black, although this is not very probable, but in any case the black whales described by him, or their descendants, are no longer ploughing the waves of the Great Bay, and our venture must apparently be classed among the hundreds of other pioneering expeditions the result of which is negative—of nearly equal value as a positive result to the world in general, but a very bitter disappointment to the particular set of pioneers.

The black whales may have changed their feeding-ground, but this does not appear likely, as the numbers of other whales still testify to the attractions of the Great Bay for this class of animals. The true explanation may be that the black whales have, since the time of Sir James, been killed in such numbers during their winter stay in warmer climates that few of them remain to go South in the summer months.

It took a long time before this conviction—of the total absence of black whales—was allowed to take possession of our minds; in the meantime, the capture of less valuable whales may go a long way towards making up for the loss.

*January* 20.—Have been steaming and sailing before a light and following breeze since yesterday. Off Cape Hallett we captured about a dozen sea-leopards lying singly on the streams of drift-ice. Tried to land at 7.30 p.m., but the steep mountain-side, wholly devoid of foreshore, looked so forbidding, and the heavy floes and bergs along the coast were moving so rapidly with the tide, that our boat had to retreat very hurriedly. Caught a few more seals during the evening. In one place off Cape Hallett, however, there appeared a beach with a penguin colony, and it may therefore be worth while to examine this situation more closely than we were able to do, before a subsequent expedition finally decides on Cape Adare as the station for wintering.

Night and day now merge into each other without appreciable change. At 11.30 p.m. the sun is high above the horizon, painting us a weirdly enchanting Antarctic picture which I must leave the pen and brush of future South Polar laureates and artists to depict in fitting words and colours. It is impossible for me to render even a moderately fair description of the other-worldly beauty and perfect uniqueness of the landscape.

The pinnacled mountains towering range beyond range in majestic grandeur under a coverlet of matchless white; the glittering and sparkling gold and silver of the sunshine, broken or reflected through the crystals of ice and snow; the sky of clearest blue and deepest gold when the sun is at its lowest; but perhaps more than all, the utter desolation, the awesome, unearthly silence pervading the whole landscape—all this combines to form a scene which is worth many a sacrifice to behold for once, although living alone in such surroundings would undoubtedly end in speedy madness.

For those who disbelieve in a 'silence which can be heard,' I will recommend a visit to South Victoria Land. When contemplating for some length of time the waste upon waste of white desolation, a remarkable sensation of monotonous, low and all-pervading chords in minor keys appears to fill your brain—a sensation which is doubtless perfectly familiar to those who have passed a day alone in a bleak mountain landscape with enormous vistas.

Turning from the mountains to the sea, the change is very great. The floating bergs and floes and the rippling or breaking waves lend an air of motion and unrest to the scene, in sharp contrast to the deathlike calm and immobility of the land, a contrast which is heightened when blowing whales, paddling seals and penguins, or wheeling petrels and gulls, introduce life as well as motion into the scenery.

Contrasting the land and sea brings out in a wonderful manner the immensity of the mountain-chains, which here attain an altitude of 14,000 feet. The stranded iceberg looks enormous as you pass close to it, and its colour strikes you as the purest white and blue, but when you look at it once more from the sea, with the South Victoria Alps in the background, it seems a very match-box, with a gray and dull surface.

The frequent showers of snow throughout the year explain the ideal whiteness of the mountains.

*January* 21.—Continued southwards in fair but cold weather. A good deal of snow had fallen in the night. Easterly breeze. Sighted Coulman Islands, completely surrounded by ice, and named the most easterly point Cape Oscar, in honour of our King and his birthday.

Before leaving Possession Islands, we had called one of the group Svend Foyn Island; another of them we named James Ross Island, as the great discoverer of South Victoria Land, with a modesty wanting in many later explorers, had strictly tabooed his own name when baptizing the numbers of islands, capes, and mountains first discovered by him. The most southerly island of the group we named Heftye's Island, after the Norwegian banker and part-owner of the vessel.

There appears to be some doubt whether in our ignorance we did not affix the name Svend Foyn Island to the one to which the name Possession Island was particularly affixed by Sir James. Should this turn out to be correct, cartographers must kindly undo the mischief, and transfer the name of our employer to the island next in importance.

No whales met with beyond one or two of the blue variety. Continued under sail and steam the whole night.

*January* 22.—Still no whales. It appeared, therefore, commercially useless to continue our voyage South, however interesting a sight would have been of Mount Erebus in possible eruption, of Mount Terror, and the great ice barrier, hundreds

of miles in length, described by Sir James Ross.
I sometimes feel that we ought to have sacrificed
a few more days, and explored the Great Bay to
the very end, to have dispelled the last chance of
illusion as regards the existence of Right whales ;
but at the time it appeared to us that the interests
of our owners demanded an immediate return in
order to give us a chance of obtaining a cargo in
other latitudes.

We went about at 8 a.m., reeling off twelve to
thirteen miles before noon, when our observation
gave us 73° 49'. At the time of turning northwards, our position was therefore 74° S. within a
mile either way.

The further we penetrated into the bay, the
more free, strange to say, it proved itself to be
as regards ice. On several occasions to-day we
could not observe even the smallest particle from
the crow's-nest. This fact, however, rather
diminished any chance of meeting whales, as the
small crustaceans and molluscs which these animals
chiefly pursue during their polar holiday are most
abundant under and between the floes.

*January* 23.—Coasting northwards again as
fast as the fresh breeze will carry us, the idea
being to explore the western shore of the main-

land and the sea towards Balleny Islands, as a
last chance of finding the lost tribe of whales. Our
second mate also thinks that our chance of finding
seals in this direction is a better one, as his Arctic
experience is unfavourable as regards the occurrence of seals off the entrance to extensive bays.
Later on we hope to explore the still more
westerly regions, where Lieutenant Wilkes fell
in with 'many' sea-elephants, should the brief
Antarctic summer allow it.

We arrived off Possession Islands at 3 p.m.,
but the new projected landing had to be abandoned on account of the strong northerly current,
which would have made it difficult to heave to in
the fresh southerly breeze.

*January* 24.—Cape Adare was made at midnight. The weather was now favourable for a
landing, and at 1 a.m. a party, including the
Captain, second mate, Mr. Borchgrevinck, and
the writer, set off, landing on a pebbly beach of
easy access, after an hour's rowing through loose
ice, negotiated without difficulty. In the calm
weather little or no swell was observable against
the shore. Jelly fish of a considerable size were
noticed in the sea, an extraordinary high latitude
for this class of invertebrate.

The sensation of being the first men who had set foot on the real Antarctic mainland was both strange and pleasurable, although Mr. Foyn would no doubt have preferred to exchange this pleasing sensation on our part for a Right whale even of small dimensions.

The tide current had been setting north with a great speed, estimated at about four to five knots an hour, but it had now turned, its velocity in the opposite direction being much less.

Our surroundings and our hosts were as strange and unique as our feelings. The latter—myriads of penguins—fairly covered the flat promontory, many acres in extent, jutting out into the bay between Cape Adare and a more westerly headland ; they further lined all accessible projections of the rocks to an altitude of 800 or 900 feet. The youngsters were now almost full-grown. In their thick, woolly, and gray down they exhibited a most remarkable and comical appearance. At a distance the confused din and screaming emanating from parents and children resembled the uproar of an excited human assembly, thousands in number.

Our presence was not much appreciated, considering the millions of years which must have elapsed since the last visit by prehistoric man or monkey—before the glacial period. Our sea-boots were bravely attacked as we passed along their ranks. The space covered by the colony was practically free from snow ; but the layer of guano was too thin, and mixed with too many pebbles, to be of commercial value in these days of cheap phosphates. Unless the guano has been carried out to sea from time to time by rains and melting snow, the thinness of the layers compared with the massiveness of similar deposits in other climes would indicate that South Victoria Land has only during comparatively recent ages been made use of by the penguins during their breeding season. From this (assumed) fact interesting inferences may again be drawn regarding changes in the climate of Antarctica during recent times, but men of science must weigh the pros and cons of this theory, and the most permissible deductions to be made.

The mortality in the colony must be frightful, judging by the number of skeletons and dead birds lying about in all directions. A raptorial (skua) gull was present here, as everywhere in the neighbourhood of penguin nurseries, and was busily occupied with its mission in life—viz., pre-vention of over-population in the colony.

The patience and endurance of the penguins are beyond praise when it is considered that thousands of them have to scale ridges hundreds of feet in height to reach their nests, although their mode of locomotion ashore is painfully awkward and slow. Like so many other polar animals, the full-grown bird is able to subsist on its own fat for long periods ; but the young birds require frequent and regular feeding, as in all other cases of animal life. The capacity of most polar inhabitants for stowing away incredible quantities of food at one meal, and bringing it up again at will, explains no doubt how the young can be fed with fair regularity, although the parents may go for days without an opportunity of eating.

To commemorate our landing, a pole was erected, carrying a box, on which was painted the Norwegian colours, the date, and the vessel's name.

Before leaving we made a collection of penguins, stones, etc. Someone had the good sense to bring a sledge-hammer, with which pieces of the original rock were detached and carried on board.

In searching the more sheltered clefts of the rock, Mr. Borchgrevinck discovered further

patches of the lichen already met with on Possession Island.   The sea-weed found on the shore
was more doubtful evidence of vegetable life, as
it may have drifted there from warmer latitudes,
although no current going South is known to me,
and no other evidence of such a current, as, for
instance, driftwood, etc., was met with.

On the shore were observed two dead seals, in
a perfectly mummified state.   I am unable to say
whether they had retired there simply to die from
wounds or disease, or had been cut off from the
open water by the ice of an early winter, and so
perished.   The hairs had all come away, but the
skins were smooth and hard, and the bodies had
kept their original form so perfectly that they
looked as if artificially preserved.

A single sea-leopard was found basking on the
shore, and killed by the Captain.   It showed no
more signs of ' uneasiness and anxiety to regain
the water ' than the two mummies.

That Antarctica can support no land mammal,
' huge ' or small, is, to my mind, proved by the
existence of these undisturbed remains.   Even
frozen seal-flesh must be a tit-bit about mid-
winter in a climate so rigorous that only the lowest
forms of vegetable life can survive from season to

season. The unbroken ice must in winter-time extend an enormous distance from the shores, driving all higher forms of animal life up to, or beyond, the edge of the open water. No land animal like the Arctic bear has ever been observed by any Antarctic traveller—the ' mysterious tracks in the snow,' etc., mentioned by one of our number were not observed by anyone else at the time—and certainly the possibility of finding Antarctic nations, etc., is too imbecile to require serious discussion.

We bade farewell about 3 a.m. to those of our hosts which we did not take away with us for a trip to natural history museums, and passed two very anxious and troublesome hours before regaining the vessel, as they had omitted to keep a look-out for us on board. We thus had the pleasure of seeing the ship working in towards the land in one direction, whilst we were compelled by the ice to take an opposite one. By shouting in chorus we at last attracted attention, and saw the course altered towards us.

The mate's excuse was the report by the man aloft that he had just observed three of us on shore going down to the boat, and so thought it best to stand in as close as possible. As we had at that time been afloat for a considerable time, this proves that penguins on the march can be easily mistaken through a telescope for human beings—at least, when Mr. M. H. is at the other end of it.

During our exploration ashore we got a strong impression that the bay at Cape Adare inside the low promontory would provide many advantages as a landing-place and station for a new expedition. It is probable, at least, that a vessel moored inside this promontory would lie protected against the outer floes, as well as the ice forming in the bay itself; the tide is no doubt very powerful along the whole shore, but presumably less so in this partly-closed bay. Among the rocks of Cape Adare, a shelter could be found for the house, and the low promontory would furnish plenty of space for moving about, for observatory, etc., as it occupies a space of about one mile in length, by a quarter of a mile in width.

The nests along the ledges prove that no avalanches have to be feared; and if by ill luck the relief-party did not succeed in fetching away the explorers during the second season, the penguin colony would afford an inexhaustible larder and stock of fuel. The bodies of the birds could be stored under the snow ; their flesh is very nourishing, if not very palatable, and their blubber yields a fuel of the highest calorific value.

In our cruise along the shores of Cape Adare we could not detect the outlying rocks described by Sir James Ross ; the only rocks we saw were close inshore, and no hindrance to navigation.

During these weeks of exciting adventures, our poor engineer, in his bunk where daylight never reaches, was compelled to content himself with our description of the wonderful and fairy-like Antarctic scenery as it opened out before us. His youth and impetuosity made the disappointment doubly bitter ; but there was absolutely no help for it, as we dared not attempt to shift him, and risk a second fracture. For another fortnight, therefore, he had to be left to sadly calculate the diameter of his swollen leg, and its slow reduction to normal proportions. When finally he was assisted on deck for the first time since the accident, mysterious Antarctica, with its snowy Alps and wonderful nights, was far beyond the southern horizon.

Nearly one-half of the seals captured during our stay in Antarctic waters exhibited, as already shortly hinted, the peculiar scars or wounds observed by previous Antarctic explorers. These wounded seals were met with throughout the pack, consequently in many cases hundreds of miles away from the nearest land; but some of the wounds were quite fresh—in fact, bleeding. The theory of a 'huge land mammal' as being the inflictor of these wounds may therefore safely be relegated to the nursery, as the scars are not found about the necks and heads of the animals, but about their body—more particularly the lower parts. The old theory that the wounds are inflicted by the fighting males in the breeding season does not appear to me very reasonable, either, in view of their position; further, their great length —up to twelve inches—and parallelism, make it wellnigh impossible that they can arise from the teeth of the seals, which are small, and arranged close together.

My personal experience of the ferocious voracity of the Icelandic ground-sharks has led me to believe that a corresponding Antarctic species of shark is responsible for the sad decimation of Antarctic seals, and that the scars referred to are inflicted on animals which have just managed to wriggle out of their iron jaws. The fondness of the Arctic shark for seal-flesh is well known;

when fishing for ground-shark, the Icelander by preference baits his hook with the flesh of a young seal steeped in brandy, concluding, no doubt, that the fluid which has so invincible an attraction for himself must be equally irresistible to the cold and damp pirate of the cod-banks. My theory has not been too well received, and I was therefore particularly delighted to find that Dr. C. Hart Merriam, in a footnote to the description of our voyage in the *Century* for January, 1896, relates as a fact that corresponding scars on the Arctic fur-seals are due to shark-bites. That a comparatively small fish should dare to attack so large an animal will be readily credible to those who know from personal experience the audacity and courage of the ground-shark, if courage can be spoken of, when sensibility is so nearly absent. When I was cod-fishing around Iceland, a shark was in one case hooked and brought alongside ; the valuable liver was removed without protest from the owner, whose sufferings I meant to end by ordering the heart and inside generally to be also cleared away before the animal was cut adrift. Imagine our consternation when the 'clean' fish on release gave a lazy wag of the tail, and went merrily to the bottom, as if much relieved by our drastic cure for any future internal complaints. Of suffering, there can have been none during the dissection, or the enormous latent strength of the fish would certainly have found expression by an attempt at struggling. I should add that even my best friends generally smile in an irritating manner when I tell them this gruesome story ; but as it is absolutely true, I shall be glad to find it circulated in order to elicit corroboratory evidence from others who can speak with the authority of practical experience. It is also a well-known fact that sharks from which the liver had been removed have been hooked and hauled up a second time ; to avoid this possibility, the Icelander blinds the fish before he lets it go. However repugnant the subject may be, it is of some importance to have our ideas of sensibility in fish readjusted by practical facts.

The Antarctic sharks may possibly, and even probably, be of a greater size than the Arctic variety ; if they are responsible for the much lesser number of seals found in Antarctic waters, they must exist in large shoals, and could no doubt be caught with suitable hooks and lines like their Arctic brethren, the liver being of great value. During my next cruise, I shall certainly make a good attempt at solving the mystery.

I have one more theory to propound in order to account for the wounds of the Antarctic seals. My personal acquaintance with the ground-shark may have caused me to undervalue the claims of another, and possibly more terrible, enemy of the seal tribe, viz., the killer or grampus (*Orca gladiator*). The courage of these dolphins is well known (three or four of them will attack the largest Right whale), and their voracity is equally phenomenal. Mr. Eschricht states that ' one of these animals was known to swallow four por-poises in succession, while from the stomach of another individual, whose length did not exceed sixteen feet, were taken fourteen seals.'

As some of my readers may have some difficulty in taking in the fourteen seals, I hasten to give my authority—' The Royal Natural History,' Frederick Warne and Co., London, 1895, vol. iii., sect. v., p. 52.

There are many arguments in favour of this second theory compared with my first. The teeth of the shark are comparatively small, and arranged in several rows ; the regular and parallel running scars, about one inch apart, are therefore not so easily explained if the shark is assumed as the enemy, whilst the few and powerful teeth of the grampus are eminently fitted for inflicting this kind of parallel gashes on an escaping seal. Whilst the existence of the Antarctic shark has still to be proved, the grampus is truly cosmopolitan ; it was observed as 'very common' near the South Polar circle by the members of the *Challenger* Expedition, swimming about in small shoals.*

I am also much afraid that the 'piebald' whales noticed by us at South Victoria Land may really have been large killers ; the collective scientific ignorance on board the *Antarctic* has left this point to be decided by the next expedition. As partial justification, it may be noted that Ross also describes small 'piebald' cetaceans, without any attempt at classification.

Although the denomination 'ground' shark must not lead anyone to suppose that this fellow inhabits exclusively the bottom of the sea, the grampus, as a genuine surface animal, has by far the best chances in his pursuit of seals. This is the last of the arguments by which I can at present support my second theory, the truth of which does

---

* 'Notes by a Naturalist,' by H. N. Moseley, p. 219 (John Murray, London, 1892).

not exclude the possibility that both grampus and shark are responsible for the scars and the small number of the seals we met with.*

The existence of a voracious shark or grampus need not, however, alone be looked to, to explain the paucity of seals in the regions we traversed compared with Arctic waters. The large continuous floes on which the seals love to congregate in large numbers were not met with during our voyage—no doubt because of the heavy swell frequently ruling where a bay runs in to the depth of 800 miles in the direction from which the prevalent gales are blowing (the wind, as a rule, blows off the ice towards you). Captain Jensen informs me that seals are not generally looked for in or close to the mouths of bays in Arctic waters, which points in the same direction. To the east and west of the great South Victoria Bay matters may improve, and larger floes may exist in more sheltered waters. The breeding season was also long past when we arrived South, and the animals were probably for this reason more scattered. We know that enormous numbers of seals have

* I have lately found that Mr. Burn-Murdoch, the illustrator of this narrative, has in his book, ' From Edinburgh to the Antarctic,' also suggested the grampus theory. I cannot therefore any longer claim it as original.

13

been caught south of Cape Horn, and further expeditions must decide whether similar multitudes do not exist in the hitherto practically unexplored waters between Graham Land and South Victoria Land. The reports by Lieutenant Wilkes point to an increase in the number of seals in a westerly direction.

If the huge land mammal existed, the seals near to the land should have been less in number than further out to sea ; but they certainly did not decrease as we worked through the pack towards the continent, and the same sleepy tameness was found everywhere—in the pack as along the shores ; I am entirely unable to corroborate the statements of a member of the expedition, that the seals found ashore 'showed uneasiness,' and 'speedily made for the water.' Three seals were met with altogether on the shore—two of them dead and mummified, as already mentioned ; and the third, a sea-leopard, sleepily happy until killed by a shot from the Captain's rifle, as already described.

I ought not to close the chapter without a reference to the remarkable variations in the force of the wind observed around South Victoria Land, but notably at Cape Adare. However boisterous the weather out at sea, close along the shores the wind was as a rule comparatively moderate.

# CHAPTER XI.

*FAREWELL TO ANTARCTICA.—FORCING THE PACK.—
SPERM WHALING.—BREAK-UP OF THE EXPEDI-
TION.*

*January* 25.—The morning had broken with
brilliant sunshine, illuminating peaks, glaciers,
and the floe-covered sea—a charming farewell
scene. Later in the day the south - easterly
breeze increased to a gale, with heavy seas and
strong intermittent showers of snow—a dangerous
combination in such close proximity to heavy floes
and bergs. The ice appeared to stretch far out
to sea, and was so firmly closed up that our chance
of working through it in a westerly direction was
rendered very doubtful.

We hove to during the worst portion of the
gale, and nearly scraped an iceberg during one
of the blinding snowfalls. Wind abated, and
fell calm as the day wore on, leaving a heavy

swell; steamed an easterly course along the edge of the pack.

*January* 26.—Sailing N.E. and E.N.E., with a light northerly breeze. The day is again fine, with occasional sunshine. Observation at noon : 69° 52′ S. lat., 169° 36′ E. long. We are therefore more easterly than Sir James Ross during his sail for Balleny.

Nothing but blue whales and a small piebald variety of finned whales are to be seen ; it therefore appears most sensible to break through the pack as fast as possible, abandoning our hopes of whaling, and to look instead for seals further west, or, in default, at Emerald and Royal Company Islands. The light northerly breeze portends a tedious battle with the ice-pack, as our coals must now be economized to the utmost. The small piebald whale may, as already stated, have been the grampus, which has a very notable erect dorsal fin, and a white blotch on each side behind the head.

*January* 27.—The same brilliant weather ; perfectly calm ; slow ahead with the engine. Much ice in all directions.

Our compasses had been considerably affected by our stay in the neighbourhood of the magnetic

WIND, BERGS, AND LOOSE ICE.

pole, and their new deviation was determined on the ice.

*January* 28.—Strong penetrating breeze from the north with snow ; much ice everywhere ; nearly beset. The floes are of a considerably larger and heavier kind than met with during our voyage south, and the blows we receive are at times alarming. Our vessel is leaking more than previously—a result, no doubt, of straining through the many collisions. We received a particularly nasty jar off Possession Island in going full tilt at a monster floe with a great way on the ship ; since then we have to give the pumps a spell during every watch, whereas formerly they were employed only night and morning.

*January* 29.—Hove to most of yesterday in foggy weather, with drifts of snow and much ice around. Steaming to-day in raw and misty weather ; ice in all directions, but not so close as to prevent our advance.

*January* 31.—Lying quiet the greater part of yesterday through foggy weather and snow, preventing all outlook. Ice everywhere ; no observation.

Considerable swell is experienced, indicating open water in the neighbourhood ; it appears to

come from the east, and our course is laid
accordingly—away from Balleny Islands. Wind
increasing to half a gale from the east in the
afternoon. Harpooned and killed with much
trouble another small Mencke whale, thus adding
to our larder another welcome supply of fresh
meat, and to our cargo about two barrels of
blubber. The capture of the whale and the
process of flensing (*i.e.*, detaching of blubber)
occupied six hours, so we must kill a great
number of this kind of whale to repay our expenses. It was astonishing to see this little
animal towing our heavy ship bravely through
the floes at the rate of about two knots, until it
was reached by some of the crew and lanced. Its
stomach was filled with the small red crustaceans
already described.

*February* 1.—Worked in a N.E. direction
among massive floes, which at times threatened
to beset us. Many violent collisions with the ice.
No observation, so we are literally 'at sea' as
regards our actual position.

Towards evening the ice slackened considerably;
large ponds opened out, and the entire horizon
from E. to N.E. showed the welcome 'water sky.'
A strong swell was noticeable from S.E. During

the whole night we progressed quickly under sail and steam through large quantities of loose ice —blocks from disintegrated bergs and floes, many of them still ponderous enough to give the vessel ugly blows.

*February* 2.—We reckon ourselves through the pack ; there are bergs and streams of large and small floes in most directions, but no unbroken pack anywhere. A lively swell from S.E. gives further proof that we are again in open sea. It is important to notice the great ease with which Sir James Ross, during his two visits, and we in 1895, broke through the ice-belt on the return voyage. The assistance to the vessel of going with the northerly current in returning, and against it in going south, is only partially explanatory of this fact. The chief reason must be the later season, during which the pack-ice has to a great extent dispersed in being carried northwards.

After the two months of nearly continuous anxiety among the ice, the change back to the heaving and rolling of the open sea was most exhilarating.

We intend to go west in search of the herds of sea-elephants described by Wilkes, but we are still without observation.

*February* 3.—Fine weather; light southerly breeze; clear water, excepting a few streams of ice and a surprising number of bergs, with which latter the sea is fairly sown. The second mate counted 250 bergs, large and small, visible at the same time from the crow's-nest; happily, there is plenty of room for us all as long as the weather keeps clear. Observation at noon: 66° 42′ S. lat. and 172° 31′ E. long. Our latitude being practically that of Balleny, we steered a westerly course. Towards night the bergs diminished in number, but many were still in sight.

*February* 4.—Light wind of S.E. Observation: 65° 25′ S. lat., 169° 31′ E. long. Under steam. Many bergs visible in the morning; fewer as the day wore on. The birds characteristic of the pack have now left us, and instead appear the common and the gray Cape pigeon, the blue and the large gray petrel, the common gull, etc., all proving that we have now left the real pack-ice behind us.

*February* 5.—Sighted Balleny or Young Island at 5 a.m. Half a gale of W.S.W.; weather clear and cold; numerous streams of ice were in sight. Observation: 66° 44′ S. lat., 167° 27′ E. long.

Hove to at 8 p.m. Sunset glorious; the lofty and imposing cone of Balleny sharply defined, with the sun dipping below the horizon behind it in a flood of gorgeous metallic colours.

The lengthening twilight already gives warning that the summer is departing; at 9 p.m. the cabin is dusky. The nights are not yet actually dark in clear weather.

*February* 7.—Wind N. E. Weather cloudy and misty; steaming and sailing with our course laid for Balleny, of which we obtain a view during a momentary clearance at noon. The land is still a considerable distance away. Afternoon almost calm; many whales around us, but all of the finned tribe; most of them like the common Arctic blue whale.

During the night we had been close up to the pack edge without observing any seals. Our chances of obtaining cargo are getting very small, as the Antarctic autumn is now drawing near.

*February* 8.—The idea of getting close under the island must be abandoned, as the weather looks threatening. The barometer is low, and the wind has increased to storm of S.W., with a heavy sea, stopping all progress and drifting us northwards.

Many bergs were seen last evening; now comparatively few. Course laid for Royal Company Islands as our last chance.

*February* 9.—Wind falling, barometer rising. A number of bergs are still surrounding us, as well as large numbers of the birds already enumerated as belonging to the open sea. Blue and other finned whales frequent. Observation, 64° 48' S. lat., 164° 8' E. long.

On the calm days the engineer is now assisted on deck, and potters round with the aid of two sticks; his time of trial is now nearly over, and the following weeks restore him to his old vigour.

*February* 10.—The day broke with glorious weather, warm sunshine, northerly breeze allowing a N.W. course. Blue and other finned whales are frequently seen by day and night. Later in the day the wind changed to storm of N.E., with a heavy sea and swell from different directions. The evening misty, with heavy blizzards of snow, rendering the navigation very dangerous on account of the bergs.

*February* 11.—Wind and sea abating during night. Observation at noon: 62° 51' S. lat., 164° 38' E. long. Steaming and sailing before a light favouring breeze.

In the evening the wind again increased to storm of S.S.W., with dense snow - showers, mountainous seas, and tremendous rolling.

*February* 12.—The wind has gone down, but we can still carry no more than reefed topsail; no ice visible. Position by calculation: 61° S. lat., 161° to 162° E. long. Strong northerly current.

*February* 13.—Wind abated to fresh breeze of N.N.W. Foggy. Westerly course. The barometer has risen to a height unusual in these latitudes—29·3″.

*February* 14.—Wind still contrary, but moderate. Weather raw and foggy. To-day's observation— unreliable on account of mist—gave us 59° 52′ S. lat.; our longitude quite uncertain.

The depression on board is not improving, and in the cabin many idle words are to be heard; but as I did not trouble to reply at the time, they may well remain unrecorded now.

*February* 15.—Contrary wind, and heavy fog in the afternoon. Northerly course for Emerald Island. Observation to-day: 60° 10′ S. lat., 157° 57′ E. long.

*February* 17.—Yesterday and to-day light westerly breeze; to-day bright sunshine, nearly calm, steaming and sailing. A brilliant Aurora

Australis evoked our admiration at night. It appeared to be descending so low as to give us the illusion of nearly touching our trucks. One member of our expedition even wished for a captive balloon so as to sample the electric fluid directly, and decide once for all its true substance, and other mysteries in connection with the auroras of both poles! Another scientific member, on coming down from the crow's-nest the next morning, declared that he had found traces of the Aurora sticking to the rigging ; it looked, he said, very much like fine spider's web! Observation at noon : 58° 15′ S. lat., 156° 15′ E. long.

*February* 18.—Fresh breeze of N.E., allowing famous progress. In the afternoon, again half a gale of W., and fog in the evening ; but we can still keep our course, or nearly so.

One of the sailors is to-day reported ill. After much consultation of medical hand-books, we diagnose his ailment as ' melancholia.' His work in the engine-room has no doubt had a bad effect on him, but, with his twenty-one years, we hope for a speedy improvement.

*February* 19.—Fine weather, westerly breeze. Observation : 55° 52′ S. lat.; longitude ' forgotten.' Steaming at night in nearly calm weather.

*February* 20.—Continued fine weather, northerly breeze, sailing and steaming four to six knots. Young This, our invalid, is far from well. Result of to-day's examination : Incipient typhoid fever. We sincerely hope that our observation of his symptoms is as wrong as ever doctors made it. Happily, the result of our diagnosis changed from day to day, no doubt according to the pages in the medical book which had been most recently read, or had made the deepest impression. Observation : 54° 17′ S. lat.

*February* 24.—Poor chance of progress during the last days. Wind from N.W., and heavy sea. To-day fine weather, with sunshine. Observation : 53° 12′ S. lat., 145° 3′ E. long. Yesterday, 54° 12′ and 146° 44′ respectively.

The welcome sight of albatrosses during the last days bears witness to the warmer latitude.

*February* 27.—Fair wind yesterday. Observation : 51° 10′ S. lat., 144° 45′ E. long. To-day again northerly wind, and little progress. Observation : 50° 27′ S. lat., and 145° 49′ E. long.

*February* 28.—Storm of N.W., with squalls, some of tremendous force ; the worst of them struck us about 2 p.m., and laid the vessel over till our lee-rail was under water, when the forestay-

sail happily blew away, and the ship righted itself.
One of our lifebuoys, marked 'Antarctic,' was
carried away, and it would be interesting to know
when and where it lands, if ever. The wind
continued equally boisterous throughout the night,
veering more westerly ; it moderated during the
next day, so that we could make sail, and lay our
course for Australia, as it appeared hopeless to
attempt to regain the neighbourhood of Royal
Company Island within a reasonable time in the
present unsettled weather, whilst the storm would
also prevent sealing should we by good luck find
the islands.

*March* 2.—Latitude 47° 51′. Fresh breeze
from S.W. The milder climate was a most
pleasant change after our months of cold.

*March* 4.—Sighted the S.E. coast of Tasmania,
to the joy and relief of everybody. We fancy we
can smell the land-air, laden with the fragrance of
apples and freshly-dug potatoes, at twenty miles
distance.

In the afternoon the wind fell nearly calm,
when to our joy and surprise we fell in with a
school of sperm whales. As by magic, all languor
and despondency vanished ; three boats were
manned and away in no time. After a few vain

FAST TO A RIGHT WHALE.

attempts, one of the school was firmly harpooned ; several of his comrades gave serious trouble in their efforts to help the wounded animal, and the falling darkness prevented us from despatching it the same night. The lines from the two harpoons were therefore carried on board and made fast, and a bad night was doubtlessly passed by the poor brute. It was killed the next morning at 7.30 with several shots and lance-thrusts, and moored alongside at 9.30, proving to be a small specimen, but very welcome, notwithstanding.

We sighted twenty to twenty-five sperm whales yesterday in several schools. It would be strange, and not a little comical, if we should have gone through all the anxiety and disappointment described in the previous chapters, and then find a cargo waiting for us practically at the entrance of the harbour from which we started.

But we appear to be thoroughly down on our luck this year. The wind sprang up again in the evening, destroying illusions and pleasant philosophizing, besides hindering us considerably in our efforts to secure the blubber ; at last the head, containing the valuable sperm-oil, was on board and safely made fast, a matter of importance in the increasing swell and rolling of the vessel.

*March* 9.—Since the 5th we have had a continual gale with nasty squalls, and seas of a magnitude sufficient to wet us through and through on the bridge itself.    Thanks to the uncommon qualities of our vessel, we have ridden out the storm without damage to speak of.    One of our boats was nearly carried away, but the crew with considerable smartness and risk got it fastened again, lashing it to the main rigging.

Yesterday the barometer showed signs of rising, and we could again lay course for Tasmania, N.W. to W.    The storm was still blowing, with heavy intermittent squalls and a confused sea. Observation : 44° 35′ S. lat., and 150° 55′ E. long., showing a surprisingly small loss of position during the gale.

To-day our latitude is 42° 31′, and immediately afterwards we sight the east coast of Tasmania, about Oyster Bay.

Of sperm whales we had seen nothing beyond a single spout during the storm, when our hands were too full for us to think of pursuit.

We ought certainly to have spent our last coals in following up the sperm whaling round Tasmania for some weeks, and so have made a last effort to recoup our employers for their heavy loss ; four or five good-sized animals would have gone very far towards this object, but the tone in the cabin had degenerated so entirely that I could not bring myself to insist on this. Every soul on board was sick of the expedition, and to a great extent of each other, and the vessel was therefore kept going towards good old Melbourne.

The pilot came on board on March 11, as we steamed and sailed at a spanking rate towards Port Phillip Heads. He brought us the latest papers. What a sensation, to be once more within the bounds of civilization and of milder climes; to feast your hungry eyes on smiling landscapes with trees, green fields, and a soft warm air all round; and, better than all, what pleasure to see the signs of human life and activity unfolding themselves as we proceed up the harbour; what a contrast to the regions of ice and snowy waste, which had for months been our only surroundings!

*March* 12.—The anchor is in the bottom; all my things are packed. As I take a last survey of the little crib in which I have passed so many waking hours, full of hope and courage to start with, then doubt and anxiety, at last settled disappointment, I cannot help reflecting how pleasant the whole cruise might have been under other

14

circumstances, how much effected to minimize, or even balance, our monetary loss, or, at any rate, to make life in adversity bearable! The worry, anxiety, and consequent mental exhaustion now make themselves severely felt. In reviewing the time occupied in our last voyage, the five and a half months appear like years, and I hasten ashore, away from the good old vessel and its memories. The physical hardships gone through have certainly been insignificant, but I feel that I would have gladly exchanged much bodily suffering in congenial society for the incessant mental racking of the last months.

At the Exchange I am greeted with the utmost cordiality by my friends, who do their best to make light of the commercial disappointment. My agent, however, receives me with the gravest news : our good old Commander has passed away during our absence, and the vessel is ordered home. This shock, coming on the top of my other tribulations, was indeed hard to bear. The telegram I had prepared to send our chief would certainly have been very different reading from my first message ; but I still believe that his stubborn toughness would have induced him, had he lived, to let me make one more effort to retrieve our misfortune, and profit by the experience bought so dearly.

The expedition was at an end; the 180 seal-skins, blubber, and sperm-oil were carried to Europe. Most of the crew left the vessel in Melbourne, and the good ship arrived in Norway after a tedious voyage of five months.

Mr. Borchgrevinck and myself had entered into a short-lived partnership in order to work up the interest for a second expedition, and whatever commercial failure we had to deplore, the colonial enthusiasm for our expedition as a voyage of exploration remained as great as ever. Our reception by the officers of the Royal Geographical Society and the Antarctic Exploration Committee was particularly cordial. At a meeting of the members at the Town Hall, addresses were delivered on the expedition itself by the writer, and on its scientific results by Mr. Borchgrevinck; and many too flattering, but still very welcome, expressions of congratulation and goodwill fell to our lot, whilst the enterprise of the owners was duly lauded.

A few days later we gave another lecture at the Athenæum Hall, under the auspices of the same two societies, His Excellency the acting

212 THE CRUISE OF THE 'ANTARCTIC'

Governor, Sir John Maddon, presiding. The Rev. W. Potter, hon. secretary to the Antarctic Committee, worked indefatigably for us in connection with this meeting. The photographs taken by me and the sketches made by Mr. Borchgrevinck were much appreciated in the form of lantern slides.

Lectures were also given by us in Sydney under the auspices of the Royal Geographical Society of New South Wales, to whose hon. treasurer, Mr. H. S. W. Crummer, we owe more than we can ever hope to repay. In Sydney I was introduced to Mr. Carruthers, Minister of the Land Department; Mr. Reid, the Premier; and several members of the Parliament, who all took a lively interest in the late voyage, and held out hopes of public support should another expedition be started from Australia.

The upshot of it all was, however, that no substantial monetary support could be found in the colonies for a new venture, and it became necessary to contemplate a canvass in Europe.

During the last weeks in Sydney, a difference between Mr. Borchgrevinck and myself had unfortunately widened until it became necessary for us to 'cut the painter.'

Into all the details of this difference, some of which are merely personal, it would serve no good purpose to enter, but as Mr. Borchgrevinck has chosen to bring it before the public, I must be allowed to state that its origin was my objection to the way in which he arrogated to himself the chief, if not the whole, credit and honour of the results of the expedition, which he joined under the circumstances set forth in a previous chapter. I confess that I consider Mr. Borchgrevinck owes me a debt of gratitude for having been permitted (at the eleventh hour) to associate himself with us at all, and that I cannot contemplate without a feeling of indignation his behaviour in hurrying back from Australia to the Geographical Congress in London, reading lectures and writing papers, wherein the promoters of the expedition and the real workers in it are mentioned only to be derided, and subsequently pursuing a similar course of conduct in my own country.

Whether that feeling is justified I must leave to the readers of these pages to determine.

# CHAPTER XII.

## *RESULTS, COMMERCIAL AND SCIENTIFIC, OF OUR EXPEDITION.*

In reviewing the results of our expedition, it is fair to give precedence to its commercial features, as our chief mission was strictly a commercial or industrial one.

We shared the fate of the great majority of industrial pioneers—to return empty-handed ; but although the direct results were negative, a careful study of the expedition will be useful to those who contemplate further ventures in Antarctic regions, indicating the paths which must in future be avoided, and also the rational way to an exploitation of these waters.

The most important negative result is the proof —bought at a cost to Norwegians of about £5,000 —that Right whales do not at present congregate in summer-time in the Antarctic pack-ice or along the shores of South Victoria Land in paying numbers from the whaler's point of view.

That my original advocacy of the expedition was, nevertheless, justified will be admitted by every unprejudiced person who reads the glowing accounts of Sir James Ross as to the numbers of Right whales met with during his two visits in 1840-41 to the same regions. I will, in self-justification, cite a few of the more important passages in his report bearing on this matter:

*Vol. i., p.* 169 : *December* 29.—'A great many whales were seen, chiefly of the common black kind, greatly resembling, but said to be distinct from, the Greenland whale ; sperm as well as hunchbacked whales were also observed. Of the common black species, we might have killed any number we pleased ; they appeared chiefly to be of unusually large size,' etc.

The latitude in this instance was about 64° S., and ice was observed in all directions.

*Vol. i., p.* 191 : *January* 14, *Lat.* 71° 50'.—'In the course of the day a great number of whales were observed ; thirty were counted at one time in various directions. . . . They were chiefly of large size, and the hunchback kind ; only a few sperm whales were distinguished amongst them.'

*Vol. i., p.* 195 : *January* 15, 71° 56′ *S. Lat.*—
'Whales also were seen in considerable numbers
during the day, and they who may hereafter seek
them in these latitudes will do well to keep near
and under the lee of extensive banks of ice,' etc.

*Vol. i., p.* 244 : *February* 17, 76° 32′ *S. Lat.*—
'A great number of whales of two different kinds
were seen, the larger kind having an extremely
long erect back-fin, while that of the smaller
species was scarcely discernible.'

*Vol. i., p.* 260 : *February* 28, 69° 57′ *S. Lat.*—
'Whales were seen in great numbers.'

*Vol. i., pp.* 265, 266 : *March* 1, *same Latitude.*—
'We saw a great many whales whenever we came
near the pack edge, chiefly of a very large size ;
and I have no doubt that before long this place
will be the frequent resort of our whaling-ships,
being at so convenient a distance from Van
Diemen's Land,' etc.

I cite the last passage to make it clear that
when Sir James, in the above as well as numerous
other instances, refers to ' whales ' without further
qualifications, he must refer to black whales, as it
would have been folly to invite his countrymen to
pursue any other kind at the time.   That he fully
realized the difference between ' whales ' (Right

whales) and 'finners' will be clear from the
further extracts of his narrative during his second
voyage :

*Vol. ii., p.* 144 : *December* 17, 61° 3″ *S. Lat.*—
' Some whales . . . were seen.'

*Vol. ii., p.* 145.—' Also a few whales of the
finner kind (were seen).'

*Vol. ii., p.* 146.—' In the evening many whales
were seen amongst the ice, and were so tame that
the ship struck upon one in passing over it.'

*Vol. ii., p.* 147 : *December* 20, 63° 23′ *S. Lat.*
(*in the Pack*).—' Numerous whales, seals . . .
were seen.'

*Vol. ii., p.* 196 : *February* 16, 75° 6″ *S. Lat.*—
' A few whales and some finners were also seen
during the day.'

*Vol. ii., p.* 208 : *February* 28, 70° 54′ *S. Lat.*—
' The small fin-backed whales, as also the piebald
kind, were numerous along the pack edge.'

What explanations can, then, be given of our
failing to observe a single Right whale during our
voyage from Campbell Islands to South Victoria
Land and back? Evidently three suppositions
are alone possible : (1) That Sir James met with
the blue (finned) whales, and mistook them for
black or Right whales ; (2) that the Right whales

have, since 1840-41, changed their route of migration ; or, finally, (3) that wholesale capture of
Right whales since 1840-41 has brought their
number down to an insignificant quantity.

The first and second suppositions are most
improbable. Sir James himself had much polar
experience ; his crew counted several practical
whalers, and the difference between the general
appearance and the spouting of finned whales and
Right whales is so striking that an error of observation continued throughout two seasons borders
on the incredible. The citations given from his
narrative prove that a distinction was made by
him between ' finners,' or ' fin-backed ' whales,
and ' whales,' or ' black whales.' When the large
number of finners with which he must have fallen
in did not excite more attention and comment,
my explanation is the utter worthlessness in his
days of the finners from a whaler's point of view ;
no means were known for the capture of these
powerful animals, and they would be looked upon
to some extent as the sportsman looks upon crows
—beneath much comment, however numerous.

The second supposition is equally feeble. The
migration of whales (like that of birds) is due to
instincts so deep-rooted that nothing but immense

physical revolutions of earth and water can be imagined to alter it; we know of no such revolutions in the South. The Antarctic regions to-day, as in 1840-41, offer the same inducements to whales in the way of a boundless food-supply, and continue to attract the finners, who take their annual summer holiday among the ice to-day as they did fifty-five years ago.

The third supposition remains, and appears to me the most plausible. The capture of Right whales in Southern latitudes previous to, and long after, the forties, was prosecuted by hundreds of vessels. Sir James mentions that 500 to 600 ships, the majority American, congregated annually round Kerguelen in pursuit of these animals; their destruction has since then proceeded with such intensity that a few whalers only in the present day can find a precarious occupation, where fifty years ago hundreds of vessels found employment.

A very little reflection will make it clear how the decimation of Right whales in a certain latitude must result in a corresponding reduction in other regions. It matters little on which point of its journey a migratory species is attacked; extermination at the winter haunts leads to extermination at all other haunts, in the case of whales as in the case of birds.

It was no doubt an accident that we failed to meet with a single one of the few remaining Right whales, which must even now seek a respite from persecution, and the materials for more blubber among the teeming crustaceans and argonautæ of the Southern ice; but our cruise should dispel the illusion of Antarctic waters as a possible field for paying Right-whaling. Some friends may consider that my reasoning suffers from obviousness, and that the same arguments should have deterred me from advocating the expedition at the outset; to these friends I reply that correct reasoning 'after the event' is particularly easy. As Right whales even now have favourite winter haunts where they are captured, it was fair to assume that they also have favourite summer haunts, and that Sir James had lighted upon one of them. Further, I reckoned with sealing and winter whaling as auxiliaries to save us from commercial failure, and it was not my fault that these resources failed.

From the above conclusion, *i.e.*, that whaling in Antarctic regions must not rely on Right whales for profit, it does not by any means follow that these latitudes have no interest to the modern whaler. It will have been noticed that hardly a day passed during our voyage without our sighting numbers of finned whales ; for many years to come these animals will form a source of great wealth to whoever sets about their capture with the same means which are employed by Norwegians at the present day, and described shortly in the second chapter of this book.

It might, indeed, be possible to copy this present mode of capture entirely, by 'fishing' with the small steamers described, from stations on the islands to the south and east of Cape Horn as a base, when the blubber could be 'tried out,' casked, and shipped home. I understand that blue whales are as plentiful in these parts as in the longitudes explored by us. Having no personal knowledge of these tracts, however, I will simply throw out the suggestion, and return to the more easterly regions, which we actually did examine. No suitable land is here sufficiently near to the whaling-grounds to afford the desirable base of operations and station for boiling the blubber, etc. The whaling expedition must therefore consist of at least two vessels—the one a small steamer, to do the actual hunting, and the other, a store ship of fair tonnage, on board which the blubber is boiled or stored in a raw state. The coals, provisions, etc., for the two vessels and their crews would also have to be carried by the store-ship.

The most practical arrangement would be to have a steamer, for the killing, of sufficient burden to keep the sea throughout the season, merely replenishing its bunkers occasionally from the store-vessel. A cheaper arrangement would be to employ for the killing a powerful launch, as large as could be carried on the deck of the store-ship without danger and excessive labour in launching and reshipping. The drawbacks to this economy would be that continuous gales might during stormy seasons interfere with the whaling where so small a craft is relied on for the actual chase; but this objection is more nominal than real, as the gales are not seriously felt among the pack, in the large ponds of which the main cargo would most likely be obtained. Intervals of idleness in respect of actual capture would also be useful in the way of clearing up and stowing the previous spoils, an affair which consumes a great deal of time. Every large iceberg also affords good shelter on the lee-side, where the hunting could proceed even in fairly boisterous weather.

By developing the shell-gun and the simultaneous attack by shell and harpoon attempted by us, I also believe it quite possible to hunt finners from a large vessel; but this is, unfortunately, only a personal belief, as the lack of experience and intelligent drill spoilt our chance in this direction on board the *Antarctic*.

An advantage in Antarctic whaling not enjoyed in Arctic regions is the possibility of employing the vessels and crews both in summer and winter: during the former season in the ice, during the latter in the warmer latitudes, where all Southern whaling has hitherto been carried on. This advantage forms an excellent foil to the disadvantage of having to transport the greater part of the oil to the Northern Hemisphere for disposal.

It would carry me beyond the proper limits of this book to detail the necessary modern gear for the capture of finners; anyone who has seen an actual Norwegian whaling-boat and harpoon-gun will have a sufficient idea of what is required. The prongs of the harpoon open out when the wounded animal bounds away and tightens the line; a glass tube containing the igniting fluid is broken by this movement of the prongs, and, coming in contact with the charge of the shell, explodes the latter, frequently killing the whale immediately.

In Arctic waters the blubber and whalebone are not the only parts of the blue whale which are utilized; the flesh is dried and used for manure. The young animals are in part laid down hermetically, and sold as 'steaks,' 'meat-balls,' and other delicacies; but in Antarctic regions the blubber would undoubtedly for some time be the only useful portion of the finner carcass. The value of a large Arctic blue whale is about £250; for the reason given, that of an Antarctic finner of the same size would be somewhat less. I have intimated that I relied on sealing and winter whaling to make up any loss due to a possible disappointment as regards finding our Right whales. Winter whaling is still carried on by a few sailing-vessels round New Zealand and Australia. There was, therefore, no valid reason why our cruise with a steamer and superior guns, etc., should not have succeeded in its object had the carrying out of my plans been in other hands; plenty of Right whales were met with, but only one secured.

Our experience at Kerguelen, and that of Scotch-men, Germans, and Norwegians round South Georgia and the South Orkneys, has proved that sealing in Antarctic regions has in it many elements of success if proper steps are taken to minimize the evil of long voyages to and from the hunting-fields. Our failure as to meeting seals in paying numbers during our voyage to the Great Bay should naturally be a warning to look for them elsewhere. The ice and lateness of the season prevented us from exploring Lieutenant Wilkes' route for seals, of which he found 'many.'

Apart from the immediate importance of Southern and Antarctic waters as sealing-grounds, I would, however, like to draw the attention of British readers to the previous immense wealth of these regions in fur-seals and sea-elephants in order to ask the question, Is it not worth Imperial attention to restore in some measure their departed glory by substituting a system of regulated capture of old and weak animals for the indiscriminate butchery of old and young, males and females, which has reduced the once important industry to such insignificant proportions?—a system akin to the one followed with such brilliant results on the Pribyloff and other islands. It would naturally

15

take a long series of years to develop a stock of anything like the old proportions; the matter is therefore one of Imperial, and not of individual, concern, unless a kind of monopoly was granted to a company.

An idea of the seal stock which these waters are capable of supporting will be obtained by the reports of Captain Weddell, of Antarctic fame, who states that the fur-seals and sea-elephants of South Georgia at the time of his visit (1823) were nearly extinct, not less than 20,000 tons of elephant-oil having been shipped to the London market alone, and not less than 1,200,000 fur-seals killed since the reports by Captain Cook, in 1771, which led sealers to this island.

South Shetland Islands were the scene of a butchery even more insane and unworthy of civilized man. During 1821 and 1822 the capture of fur-seals is computed at 320,000, the animal becoming nearly extinct after the second year, the motherless young dying by tens of thousands, when judicious regulations and selection of animals to be killed would have allowed 100,000 skins to be secured annually for a long period without seriously decreasing the stock. How it is possible to practically exterminate in two years the whole stock of a vast region is explained by the peculiar habits of the fur-seal, which it would carry me too far to explain here in detail to the non-practical reader. Practically all fur-seals, inhabiting large areas, repair annually to the nearest land, either for breeding purposes or for renewing their coats of hair. A party stationed all the year round on this land, and killing off every animal as it comes ashore, has it therefore in its power to virtually exterminate the seals over large areas of their watery habitat.

The same policy of indiscriminate slaughter followed at Kerguelen has had the same result— nearly complete extermination of seals, fur-seals in particular ; our comparative success was no doubt due to the fact that the island had not for some years been visited by sealers, giving the poor animals a chance of peaceful multiplication.

The close season adopted on Campbell and Auckland Islands is no doubt better than nothing ; but to attain really great results, the killing of seals must be wholly prevented at all times of the year *on the lands chosen by them for breeding,* except such regulated and selective killing as in the Pribyloff Islands. This perennial closing of breeding-grounds might entail some hardship on vested interests, which might have to be conciliated ; but large hunting - fields would still remain open in the ice-fields, giving a fair scope to new enterprise. Even there, an internationally accepted close season, as arranged in the Arctic waters, might be of great advantage to the sealers themselves.

Having treated (at perhaps too great length) the question of Antarctic sealing and whaling as the most interesting theme to the practical man, I will shortly enumerate the somewhat poor additions to natural science made through our expedition, a poverty explained by the absence on board of anyone of fair scientific attainments, through the deplorable failure on the part of Mr. Bruce to reach us before our start from Melbourne.

The discovery of most interest to botanists was no doubt the finding on Possession Island, and later on at Cape Adare, of a lichen growing sparsely in sheltered nooks. As it was previously held that no vegetation, even of the lowest order, was possible in the rigorous clime of Antarctica, this interesting lichen has created a great sensation.

Some of the seaweed collected at Cape Adare was also carried to Europe, and it may still be proved that it was actually growing where found ;

if so, the number of Antarctic botanic species will be doubled—there will be two instead of one.

To the zoology of Antarctica we made no fresh addition, the earless seal being already described by others. On Campbell Islands a new and graceful species of wader was shot by Mr. Borchgrevinck, but this can hardly be classed as an addition to Antarctic fauna, however interesting in other respects. The discovery of jelly fish at Cape Adare may be novel in so high a latitude.

The ice island described as Svend Foyn Island is, as far as I know, the greatest mass of floating ice ever met with, and for this reason worth attention. The extracts from the log of the *Antarctic*, and the notes in the previous pages, will give information as regards the condition of Antarctic ice in 1894-95, which may be of value to geographers and to those contemplating similar expeditions. The chief feature as regards the ice is the very high latitudes in which we fell in with the first bergs, as will be observed from the log. I had collected a number of observations from other voyages to illustrate this, but find the matter of Antarctic ice dealt with so exhaustively by scientists, quoting hundreds of observations, that I hastily abandoned all efforts to instruct where the facts are already so well known.

Although the breadth of the ice-pack traversed by us—500 miles—was greater than that met with in January, 1840, by Sir James Ross, it was 300 miles less in breadth than the belt which it took him fifty-six days to break through in December, 1840—February, 1841. We must therefore look upon 1894-95 as an average year in respect of Antarctic ice; with a heavier vessel and stronger engine, we should no doubt have worked our way through in a much shorter time.

The most interesting feature of the ice was its firmer and more closely packed state compared with 1840-41. During the latter years the swell penetrated to the very heart of the pack, and nearly wrecked the explorers on one occasion through the violent blows of the floes ; whilst gale after gale was ridden off by us in perfect comfort, the swell, as a rule, being at most the very gentlest undulation as soon as we had got well into the ice. The daily observations during our passage through the ice will have shown that the floes increased very much in bulkiness as we worked towards Antarctica. This shows that no great intermixing of the ice takes place until it reaches higher latitudes ; the floes drift northwards for an enormous distance in the same order as they break away and get afloat.

Of new geographical discoveries, we made few of any importance beyond the actual landing at Cape Adare and examination of the nearest parts. The samples of rock brought back by us from the mainland have been distributed among various societies. Captain Bernhard Jensen, our second mate, submitted his samples to Dr. John Murray, by whose kind intervention the exhaustive description by Mr. J. J. H. Teall in Appendix II. has been secured. For Mr. Teall's extreme kindness in undertaking this work and permitting the publication of his results I must be allowed herewith to tender my very best thanks.

As we followed another explorer's track and made no original discoveries of land, we abstained from any extensive naming of capes, islands, etc. In fact, the only names affixed during the cruise by the Captain and myself were the following :

Cape Oscar to the eastern point of Coulman Island.

Svend Foyn Island to the northern island of the Possession Group.

Ross Island to the next one of the same group,

where Sir James was supposed to have landed in 1840. The possible error committed by us in this naming has been referred to in Chapter X.

Cape von Mueller to the east cape of Possession Island, in honour of the world-famed botanist of that name, and to commemorate the valuable find of lichen in this island.

Heftye's Island, to the southernmost of the Possession Group, in honour of Messrs. Thos. Joh. Heftye and Son, of Christiania, the only shareholders in the *Antarctic* besides Mr. Foyn.

I hope that the British Admiralty will think our claim sufficient to have these names adopted.

An exact copy of a tracing by Sir James Ross had been presented to me by Mr. H. S. W. Crummer, of the N.S.W. Royal Geographical Society, previous to our voyage. I was much amused to subsequently receive a copy of a chart by Captain Kristensen—an exact copy of the above tracing—illustrating our track, and studded with new names of capes, peaks, etc. As all these names were affixed by the Captain at *Melbourne*, with the assistance of a local friend, I hold that this way of baptism, thousands of miles away from the infant to be christened, is not quite proper, and that 'Potter Peninsula,' etc., have little right to appear on any chart. For the same reason I have no desire that the name ' Bull's Rocks' shall appear on any chart, as this kind of log-rolling and self-immortalization is particularly distasteful to me. The loss of immortality to myself, the Rev. Mr. Potter and his friends, can be rectified by a subsequent expedition resulting in more original discoveries.

Our expedition has in many respects paved the way for a better equipped venture; we have proved that landing on Antarctica proper is not so difficult as it was hitherto considered, and that a wintering-party have every chance of spending a safe and pleasant twelvemonth at Cape Adare, with a fair chance of penetrating to, or nearly to, the magnetic pole by the aid of sledges and Norwegian *ski-es*.

Finally, our expedition has given a fresh and strong impulse to Antarctic exploration in general, and I flatter myself that the comparative ease— viewed as an exploring expedition—with which we succeeded in penetrating the dreaded ice-belt has had much to do with the several European expeditions now preparing or in contemplation. Although the existence of land mammals, ' huge ' or small, of new races, etc., in Antarctica is truly a physical impossibility, its millions of unexplored square miles offer problems of the most fascinating character to the meteorologist, geologist, and geographer. The highest authorities affirm that many of the most important questions in terrestrial magnetism and physical geography generally must remain doubtful until exploration parties have made the necessary observations throughout the year in various points of Antarctica. The shores have some interest to the botanist, and offer an immense field to the zoologist, particularly to the student of the marine forms of life. A vast number of new species of fishes await classification, and the seas are proved to be simply teeming with the lower forms of animal life.

I do not know whether it will ever be my lot to revisit Antarctica, but the years spent in realizing my dream of an Antarctic expedition will ever remain among the most pleasant, certainly the most interesting, part of my life, disappointments and tribulations notwithstanding.

# APPENDIX I.

## EXTRACTS FROM THE LOG OF THE 'ANTARCTIC.'

Meteorological Observations on board the Steam-Whaler 'Antarctic' during November, 1894.

| Day. | Position. Lat. S. | Position. Long. E. | Temperature. Air. | Temperature. Water. | Barometer. | Wind. Direction. | Wind. Force. | Weather. |
|---|---|---|---|---|---|---|---|---|
| 2 | 54° 44' | 166° 6' | 50° & 47° | 46° | 29·1 | N.W. | 6 | Cloudy; rain. |
| 3 | 55 32 | 167 12 | 48 & 42 | 44 | 29·2 | S.S.E. | 3 | Overcast. |
| 4 | 56 16 | 163 50 | 42 & 38 | 44° & 38° | 29·6 | S E. & W.N.W. | very light | Very fine. |
| 5 | 57 34 | 162 40 | 41 & 39 | 34 & 32 | 28·7 | W.N.W. | 7 to 9 | Gray and cloudy; sighted the first [iceberg. |
| 6 | 58 14 | 162 35 | 41 & 40 | 34 & 32 | 28·6 | N. | 6 | Fog and clear. |
| 7 | 59 8 | 163 50 | 42° | 34° | 28·8 | N.W. | 2 | Fine and overcast. |
| 8 | 59 8 | 163 35 | 42 | 34 | 28·7 | N.N.W. | 3 | Fine. |
| 9 | 58 49 | 164 10 | 40 & 39 | 34 & 34 | 28·7 | N.W. & W. | 2 | Cloudy. |
| 10 | 57 56 | 165 21 | 40 & 40 | 38 & 38 | 28·3 | S.E. | 8 | Cloudy. |
| 11 | 54 58 | 165 15 | 41 & 41 | 38° | | S. & S.W. | 8 | Stormy. |
| 12 | 53 50 | 165 3 | 50° | 38 | 28·4 | N. | 5 | Cloudy. |
| 13 | 50 56 | 164 38 | 45 | 44 | 29·6 | S. | 9 | Cloudy. |
| 14 | 48 44 | 165 41 | 49 | 44 | 28·8 | W. | 5 | Gray. |

Sighted the Snares off New Zealand.

OBS.—On November 7 we got our propeller out of order, so had to go back to Port Chalmers, New Zealand, which port was reached on November 18, and left again on November 23, 1894.

OBS.—We left Campbell Island on October 31, going southwards, as above position shows.

OBS.—The force of the wind is indicated by the figures from o=calm, to 12=hurricane.

## Meteorological Observations on board the Steam-Whaler 'Antarctic' during December, 1894.

| Day. | Lat. S. | Long. E. | Air. | Water. | Barometer. | Direction. | Force. | Weather. |
|---|---|---|---|---|---|---|---|---|
| 1 | 54° 33' | 165° 11' | 50° | 48° | 28·8 | W. & N.W. | 6 & 5 | Fine ; clear. |
| 2 | 56 41 | 165 28 | 42 | 44° & 44° | 29·2 | S.W. & W. | 6 & 7 | Fine ; p.m. gray. |
| 3 | 58 41 | 166 41 | 42° & 42° | 40 & 40 | 29·2 | W.S.W. | 6 & 7 | Icebergs sighted. |
| 4 | 61 11 | 168 53 | 42 & 40 | 38 & 38 | 28·9 | N.W. | light | Fewer icebergs ; fine weather. |
| 5 | 63 3 | 169 18 | 38 & 38 | 32 & 32 | 29·2 | N.N.W. | 5 | Clear ; fog of short duration. |
| 6 | 64 44 | 168 58 | 35 & 35 | 30 & 30 | 28·9 | N.W. & W. | 5 | |
| 7 | 65 11 | 168 39 | 35 & 34 | 30° | 29 | N.W. | 5 | Heavy snowfall. |
| 8 | 65 45 | 171 36 | 35 & 35 | 28 & 28 | 28·6 | N.W. | 7 | Gray ; much snow ; running into the ice-pack. |
| 9 | 66 46 | 171 36 | 35 & 32 | 28 & 28 | 28·3 | W.N.W. | 7 | Thick ; clearing in the pack. |
| 10 | 66 48 | 171 36 | 30 & 29 | 28 & 28 | 28·7 & 28·3 | N.E. | 5 | Clear and thick ; threatening. |
| 11 | 66 48 | 171 36 | 32 & 30 | 28° | 28·5 | S.W. | 9 | |
| 12 | 65 29 | 166 37 | 35 & 34 | 28 | 28·7 | S. | 9 | |
| 13 | 65 40 | 163 53 | 30 & 30 | 30 & 30 | 28·6 | calm | 2 | Overcast. |
| 14 | 65 40 | 163 53 | 32 & 31 | 30° | 28·6 | calm | 2 | |
| 15 | 65 58 | 164 10 | 32 & 32 | 28 & 28 | 28·8 | W. | 4 | At 7 p.m. sighted Balleny Island in south. |
| 16 | 65 58 | 164 10 | 35 & 35 | 28 & 28 | 28·8 | N.W. & N. | 6 | Overcast. |
| 17 | 65 58 | 164 10 | 34° | 28° | 28·6 | N.W. to W. | 9 | Clearing. |
| 18 | 65 58 | 164 10 | 35 | 30 | 28·7 | calm | 2 | Overcast ; clearing. |
| 19 | 66 14 | 165 10 | 35 | 30 | 28·8 | S.S.W. | 1 | Half overcast ; clearing. |
| 20 | 66 15 | 165 45 | 34 & 32 | 30 | 28·8 | N.W. | 5 | Fine ; clear. |
| 21 | 66 13 | 165 5 | 32° | 30 | 28·7 | calm W.N.W. | 5 | Fine ; overcast. |
| 22 | 66 8 | 167 37 | 34 | 30 | 29 | S.W. | 4 | Clear ; bright. |
| 23 | 66 11 | 169 28 | 35 & 31 | 28 & 28 | 29 | N.W. | 3 | Fine ; clear. |
| 24 | 66 33 | 170 19 | 32 & 30 | 28 & 28 | 29 | S.W. | 5 | Cloudy ; stormy. |
| 25 | 66 32 | 170 25 | 32 & 32 | 28 & 28 | 28·6 | E. | 4 | Overcast ; clear. |
| 26 | 66 55 | 170 40 | 32° | 28° | 28·8 | W. | 6 | Heavy squalls. |
| 27 | 66 37 | 171 15 | 32 | 28 | 28·7 | W. | 9 | Overcast ; clear. |
| 28 | 66 47 | 171 49 | 32 | 28 & 28 | 28·8 | W. | 2 | Overcast ; clear. |
| 29 | 66 56 | 172 46 | 32 | 28 & 28 | 29 | W. | 1 | Fine ; clear. |
| 30 | 66 52 | 173 8 | 30 | 28 & 28 | 29·2 | W. | 5 | Fine ; clear. |
| 31 | 66 47 | 174 13 | 30 | 28 & 28 | 29 | W.S.W. | 4 | Overcast. |

## Meteorological Observations on board the Steam-Whaler 'Antarctic' during January, 1895.

| Day | Lat. S. | Long. E. | Air | Water | Barometer | Direction | Force | Weather |
|---|---|---|---|---|---|---|---|---|
| 1 | 66° 50' | 175° 45' | 33° | 28° | 28·8 | W. | 4 | Strong snowfall. |
| 2 | 67 5 | 175 45 | 33 | 28 | 28·8 | W. & N.W. | 4 to 10 | Storm during night. |
| 3 | 67 20 | 176 31 | 34° & 31° | 28° & 28° | 28·8 | W. | 6 | Overcast. |
| 4 | 67 20 | | 30 & 29 | 28 & 28 | 28·7 | N.W. | 5 | Overcast; snow. |
| 5 | 67 23 | | 30 & 30 | 28 & 28 | 28·7 | S.W. | 7 | Overcast. |
| 6 | 67 42 | | 32 & 32 | 28° | 28·9 | S.W. | 4 | Overcast. |
| 7 | 68 6 | 177 20 | 32° | 28 & 28 | 29 | S.W. | 2 to 0 | Overcast. |
| 8 | 68 6 | 177 20 | 28 & 28 | 28 & 28 | 28·9 | E. | 8 | Heavy squalls; snow. |
| 9 | 68 21 | 176 15 | 27° | 28 & 28 | 28·6 | E. | 8 | Clear. |
| 10 | 68 7 | | 27 & 29 | 28 & 28 | 28·6 | S. | 9, 10 | Overcast. |
| 11 | | | 30° | 28 & 28 | 28·2 | W. | 6 | Overcast. |
| 12 | 68 7 | 176 59 | 32 & 28 | 28 & 28 | 28·3 | S. | 5 | Clear. |
| 13 | 68 12 | 177 30 | 31° | 28° | 28·6 | S. | 5 | Clear. |
| 14 | 69 16 | 175 19 | 32 & 30 | 28 & 28 | 28·6 | W. | 4 | Clear; came into open water. |
| 15 | 70 18 | 171 10 | 36 & 31 | 29 & 30 | 28·7 | N.E. | 1 | Clear; beautiful. |
| 16 | 71 12 | 170 18 | 32 & 32 | 29° | 28·7 & 29 | N.E. | 7 | Clear; sighted Victoria Land. |
| 17 | 71 45 | | 36 & 32 | 30 & 30 | 29 & 28·7 | S.E. | 7 | |
| 18 | | | 35° | 29° | 28·9 | S.W. | 4 | Clear; sailing; land in sight. |
| 19 | | | 35 | 29 | 28·8 | calm | 2 | Clear; steering southwards. |
| 20 | | | 31 & 30 | 29 | 28·8 | calm | 1 | Overcast. |
| 21 | 73 8 | | 32 & 30 | 29 & 29 | 28·9 | S. | | Overcast; off Coulman Island. |
| 22 | 73 49 | | 30° | 29° | 29 | S.S.E. | 4 | Steering northwards. |
| 23 | 72 01 | | 32 | 29 | 29·2 | N.E. | 5 | Overcast; landed at Cape Adare. |
| 24 | 71 3 | 169 36 | 30 & 30 | 29 | 29·2 | E. | 3 | Overcast; heavy snowfall. |
| 25 | 70 24 | 170 14 | 30 & 30 | 29 | 28·8 | N. | 9 | Overcast; clear. |
| 26 | 69 5? | 170 57 | 32 & 31 | 30 & 30 | 29 | calm | 4 | Overcast; re-entered the ice-pack. |
| 27 | 69 44 | | 30 & 30 | 28 & 28 | 28·7 | N. | | Overcast. |
| 28 | 68 56 | | 34° | 29 & 29 | 29·1 | N. | 4 | Overcast; snow. |
| 29 | 68 56 | | 34 | 29° | 29 | N. | 2 | Overcast. |
| 30 | 68 7 | 170 41 | 34 & 33 | 28 & 28 | 28·9 | N. | 1 | Overcast. |
| 31 | | | 33 & 34 | 28 & 28 | 29 | N.E. | 1 | Overcast. |

## Meteorological Observations on board the Steam-Whaler 'Antarctic' during February, 1895.

| Day. | Position. | | Temperature. | | Barometer. | Wind. | | Weather. |
|---|---|---|---|---|---|---|---|---|
| | Lat. S. | Long. E. | Air. | Water. | | Direction. | Force. | |
| 1 | 68° 49' | 172° 40' | 31° & 32° | 28° & 28° | 28·6 | S.E. | 3 | Come into open water; overcast. |
| 2 | 69 48 | 173 51 | 30° | 28° | 28·9 | S.E. | 5 | Overcast. |
| 3 | 66 42 | 172 31 | 31 & 31 | 28 | 28·7 | S.E. | 4 | Clear; overcast. |
| 4 | 65 24 | 169 27 | 32 & 34 | 30 & 30 | 28·7 | S.E. | 5 | Strong snowfall. |
| 5 | 65 44 | 167 8 | 32° | 30 & 30 | 28·7 | W.S.W. | 6 | Overcast. |
| 6 | 66 34 | 166 24 | 32 & 32 | 30 & 30 | | N.E. | 6 | Foggy. |
| 7 | 66 34 | 165 44 | 34° | 30 & 30 | 28·5 | N.E. | 3 | Snow. |
| 8 | 65 22 | 164 8 | 33 | 30° | 28·2 | S.W. | 8 | Overcast; gloomy. |
| 9 | 64 48 | 164 38 | 34 & 32 | 30 & 30 | 28·5 | W.S.W. | 6 | Overcast; snow; clear. |
| 10 | 63 22 | 164 33 | 40° | 30° | 29 | N. | 5 | Clear. |
| 11 | 62 51 | 158 48 | 35 & 35 | 30 & 30 | 28·5 | N.N.E. | 6 | Overcast; snow. |
| 12 | 61 11 | 157 51 | 35° | 34 | 29·1, rising | S.W. | 11 | Overcast; half-clear. |
| 13 | 61 36 | 156 57 | 36 | 34 | 29·2 | S.W. | 5 | Overcast; half-clear; foggy. |
| 14 | 59 52 | 156 53 | 38 | 34 | 29·3 | W. | 5 | Overcast; half-clear; foggy. |
| 15 | 60 10 | 157 15 | 40 | 35 | 29·3 | W. | 7 | Half-overcast. |
| 16 | 58 48 | 156 59 | 40 | 34 | 29·2 | W. | 4 | Half-overcast. |
| 17 | 58 15 | 156 17 | 43 | 37 | 29·3 | W. | 3 | Half-overcast; strong Aurora Australis; clear. |
| 18 | 56 53 | 153 9 | 42 | 37 | 29·4 | N.E. | 4 | Half-overcast; Aurora Australis; clear. |
| 19 | 55 52 | 152 1 | 41 | 37 | 29 | W. | 7 | Clear; overcast. |
| 20 | 54 17 | 151 9 | 44 | 40 | 29·3 | W. | 3 | Clear. |
| 21 | 53 34 | 148 1 | 46 | 40 | 29·4 | N.W. | 4 | Clear. |
| 22 | 53 32 | 147 37 | 46 | 40 | 29·3 | N.W. | 7 | Overcast. |
| 23 | 54 12 | 146 44 | 39 | 40 | 29·2 | N.W. | 6 | Clear. |
| 24 | 53 12 | 146 36 | 44 | 40 | 29·1 | N.N.W. | 4 | Clear; overcast. |
| 25 | 51 42 | 144 9 | 44 | 40 | 29·1 | N. | 5 | Overcast; half-clear. |
| 26 | 51 10 | 145 28 | 44 | 40 | 29 | S.W. | 5 to 8 | Clear; overcast. |
| 27 | 50 27 | 145 49 | 42 | 40 | 29·4 | N.W. | 6 | Overcast. |
| 28 | 50 56 | 143 8 | 45 | 40 | 28·8 | N.W. | 10 to 12 | Very heavy weather. |

Meteorological Observations on board the Steam-Whaler 'Antarctic' during March, 1895.

| Day. | Position. | | Temperature. | | Barometer. | Wind. | | Weather. |
|---|---|---|---|---|---|---|---|---|
| | Lat. S. | Long. E. | Air. | Water. | | Direction. | Force. | |
| 1 | 50° 34' | 145° 27' | 45° | 40° | 28·7 | S.W. | 10 | Overcast ; clear. |
| 2 | 47 51 | 143 20 | 47 | 45 | 29·4 | S.W. | 7 | Overcast ; clear. |
| 3 | 45 56 | 146 27 | 55 | 50 | 29·9 | W. | 5 | Clear ; sighted Tasmania. |
| 4 | 44 35 | 147 54 | 50 | 50 | 29·8 | N.N.W. | 6 | Overcast. |

*March 4 and 5.*—Were working with a sperm whale.
*March 6, 7 and 8.*—Had very strong gale from west, with a heavy, confused sea. Barometer 29 to 29·4.
*March 9.*—Sighted again Tasmania ; arrived in Melbourne on March 12, 1895.

H. J. BULL.

# APPENDIX II.

### NOTES ON SPECIMENS FROM POSSESSION ISLAND AND CAPE ADARE, COLLECTED BY CAPTAIN JENSEN.

'These stones are from Possession Island, taken from the rock—excepting the two hard specimens which are from Cape Adare, South Victoria Land— and picked up by me on January 24, 1895.'—NOTE BY CAPTAIN JENSEN.

THE collection includes eleven specimens from Possession Island and two from Cape Adare. Those from Possession Island are formed of a vesicular igneous rock which varies in colour from dark gray to almost black. Several have their exposed surfaces coated with a laminated deposit, about an eighth of an inch thick, of compact white or cream-coloured phosphate (guano), doubtless formed from the droppings of sea-birds. The vesicles vary in size in different specimens, and even in different portions of the same specimen. The smallest are only recognisable under the microscope, whereas the largest are a quarter of an inch or more in diameter. They also vary in abundance. In some specimens they are so numerous that the actual rock is reduced to thin honeycomb-like partitions separating contiguous cavities. Such specimens will only just sink in water, and it may be safely inferred that pumice capable of floating was produced in connection with the eruptions which gave rise to this rock.

Microscopic sections prepared from the more compact specimens show that the rock is composed of a few scattered phenocrysts of augite and hornblende in a ground-mass of lath-shaped basic plagioclase, granular augite, magnetite, and a little pale-brown glass crowded with specks of iron-ore and extremely minute colourless microlites.

The augite-phenocrysts are pale brown in colour, and, although often occurring as crystal fragments, show no signs of corrosion. The external boundaries of the individuals are either crystalline faces or fractured surfaces meeting in sharp angles. The phenocrysts of hornblende, on the other hand, show marked signs of corrosion. Their angles have usually been rounded off, and they are often elliptical in outline. They are also usually surrounded by the well-known aureole, rich in magnetite, which is the characteristic indication of the corrosive action of the magma. In their section they are seen to be strongly pleochroic in pale yellowish brown and deep brown tints. Both in colour and mode of occurrence they resemble the hornblende of the basalts described by Sommerlad* from the Rhön and Westerwald. The constituents of the ground-mass do not require detailed description.

The most compact specimen on which the above description is mainly based is evidently a lava, but it contains one or two vesicular lapilli which either fell on the stream during its flow, or, as is perhaps more probable, resulted from the breaking up of the first formed and more vesicular portions of the stream itself.

The rock is a non-olivine-bearing hornblende-basalt. All the specimens from Possession Island are of the same general type, but in the more highly vesicular varieties the constituents of the ground-mass, with the exception of some of the larger felspars, which should perhaps be regarded as phenocrysts, have not been so distinctly individualized.

The two specimens from Cape Adare belong to two very different types of rock. The larger one, measuring about five inches in its longest diameter, is a brown compact igneous rock, having a specific gravity of 2·75. Under the microscope it is seen to consist of a few minute phenocrysts of a pale-coloured augite and irregular opaque patches of iron-ore in a

* 'Ueber Hornblendfuhrende Basaltgesteine :' 'Neues Jahrbuch.' Beilage, Band II., p. 139.

16

ground-mass composed of felspar-microlites, grains and crystals of magnetite, microlites of augite, and a colourless, feebly polarizing base. There are also numerous excessively minute prismatic, colourless microlites, which cannot be definitely identified, but which are undoubtedly similar to those occurring in the hornblende-basalt from Possession Island. The main interest of this specimen centres in the colourless substance which forms the ultimate base of the rock. This may be largely decomposed by cold hydrochloric acid, and when portions of the liquid are removed from the surface of the thin section by means of a capillary tube, transferred to a clean glass slip, and allowed to evaporate, crystals of common salt make their appearance in abundance. Moreover, the portions of the slide which have been acted upon by the acid can be stained with fuchsine in consequence of the formation of gelatinous silica. These facts prove that the colourless substance is largely, if not entirely, formed of nepheline, and that the rock is a nepheline-tephrite.

The hornblende-basalt of Possession Island and the nepheline-tephrite from Cape Adare are both of them volcanic rocks of comparatively recent date. Similar rocks occur in North Germany, where they show a tendency to pass into each other;* but such rocks are unknown in the Brito-Icelandic Province. It is interesting to note that nepheline has been described by Max Hartman,† on somewhat doubtful evidence, as occurring in some of the basalts of the Auckland Islands, which lie to the south of New Zealand, and on approximately the same longitude as South Victoria Land. The distance between the Auckland Islands and Cape Adare is very great; but having regard to the extensive areas over which the volcanic rocks of one period are known to maintain their distinctive characters, it is by no means improbable that the Auckland Islands and South Victoria Land belong to the same petrographical province.

* Rosenbusch: 'Mikroskopische Physiographie der massigen Gesteine.' 2nd edition, p. 739.

† 'Ueber Basalte der Auckland's Inseln:' 'Neues Jahrbuch,' 1878, p. 825.

The other specimen from Cape Adare is a pebble, half of which is formed of vein quartz, and the other half of a granitic rock which has been crushed by earth movements and more or less recemented by quartz. This rock must at one time have formed part of an extensive tract of land; but, seeing that it is a pebble, we are unable to say whether it came from the supposed Antarctic Continent or from some region to the north.

J. J. H. TEALL.

*March* 18, 1896.

THE END,

BILLING AND SONS, PRINTERS, GUILDFORD.

For EU product safety concerns, contact us at Calle de José Abascal, 56–1°, 28003 Madrid, Spain or eugpsr@cambridge.org.

 www.ingramcontent.com/pod-product-compliance
Ingram Content Group UK Ltd.
Pitfield, Milton Keynes, MK11 3LW, UK
UKHW010345140625
459647UK00010B/828